SPICE UP YOUR LIFE WITH JOY

Spice Up Your Life with Joy

SANDY PETRO

VICTOR BOOKS®

A DIVISION OF SCRIPTURE PRESS PUBLICATIONS INC.
USA CANADA ENGLAND

Recommended Dewey Decimal Classification: 227.6
Suggested Subject Heading: BIBLE, N.T., EPISTLES—PHILIPPIANS

Library of Congress Catalog Card Number: 90-081687
ISBN: 0-89693-817-4

1 2 3 4 5 6 7 8 9 10 Printing/Year 94 93 92 91 90

VICTOR BOOKS
A division of SP Publications, Inc.
Wheaton, Illinois 60187

What recipe for life are you following? How has that recipe been turning out? Are you happy? Is your life full of rich flavors that leave you satisfied, or is it more on the bland side with something apparently missing? Are you anxious to taste the freshness of each new day, or does each day offer you leftovers from the day before?

In Philippians, Paul gives us a recipe for life that never fails regardless of daily circumstances. He both shows us and tells us how to "spice up our lives with joy."

In order for a recipe to turn out successfully, you must have the right ingredients and must follow the directions precisely. This study will guide you to discover for yourself the ingredients of Paul's joy as found in God's Word. You will then be given directions for applying God's truths to your life in such a way that your joy will be increased and made more complete.

Usually when we try a recipe, we want it to be recommended by someone we know and trust. Jesus Himself recommends joy to all His disciples. In fact, joy was one of the topics of conversation between Jesus and His disciples in the Upper Room! In John 15:11 Jesus says, "I have told you this so that My joy may be in you and that your joy may be complete" (NIV). In John 16:24 Jesus says, "Until now you have not asked for anything in My name. Ask and you will receive, and your joy will be complete" (NIV). In John 17:13 Jesus says, "I am coming to you now, but I say these things while I am still in the world so that they may have the full measure of My joy within them" (NIV).

Jesus Christ is mentioned dozens of times in the 104 verses of Philippians. This frequent emphasis on Christ makes us realize that He is the basis of Paul's joy. Therefore, you will need to taste of Christ Himself before you will be able to taste the full flavor of Paul's recipe. This study will enable you to do so and, as a result, you will experience increased victory in your life through newly gained confidence in Christ!

Each chapter of this study is divided into three sections. The first section, "Simmer These Thoughts," is designed to help you discover for yourself what the Scripture passage is saying. It contains thought-provoking questions which will help you examine and interpret God's Word. The second section, "Savor God's Truth," is designed to be read after you have completed the first section. Its purpose is to expand the theme and spiritual concepts found in "Simmer These Thoughts." The third section, "Season Your Life," challenges you to action. It suggests practical ways to personally apply God's Word to your life and the lives of others.

Spice Up Your Life with Joy can be used as an individual personal Bible study, or it can be used as a group study. A resource section titled "Leader's Recipes" has been added as an aid for anyone desiring to lead a group through this study.

May your joy increase and be made complete as you use this study as a tool for understanding and experiencing the infallible Word of God!

CHAPTER ONE

Joyful Prayer

❧ SIMMER THESE THOUGHTS ❧

Read Acts 16:1-40.
1. What is Paul's relationship to Philippi and the Philippians? How would 1 Corinthians 4:14-17 relate to your answer?

2. What is Timothy's relationship to Paul? To the Philippians?

3. Compare and contrast the lives of Paul's first three converts in Philippi. How do these conversions relate to James 2:1-8?

Read Philippians 1:1-11.
4. How does Paul identify himself? What qualities does a servant possess? What is involved in being a true servant of God?

5. To whom is Paul writing? What are the qualifications of a saint?

9

Read 1 Corinthians 1:2. Are you a saint?

6. How would you define "joy"? What is the source of Paul's joy? What is your source of joy? Compare and contrast "joyfulness" and "happiness."

7. "Grace and peace" is a familiar blessing used by Paul in his letters to his churches. What do these words mean to you? Have you experienced grace and peace as portrayed in Romans 5:1-9?

8. What phrase in Philippians 1:5 accounts for the closeness between Paul and the Philippian Christians? What does this phrase mean to you?

9. Of what is Paul confident in verse 6? Define what he means by "good work" in this verse. Can we share this same confidence? Explain.

10. What does verse 7 reveal about the Philippians' relationship with Paul? Read Philippians 4:14-18 for additional insight.

11. Name four specific goals from Philippians 1:9-11 that Paul desires for the Philippians. From these four goals, what should be the Philippians' ultimate goal for their spiritual growth? Apply this goal to your own life.

12. In light of verse 9, what would Paul think about the idea that "love is blind"?

13. What are the fruits of righteousness, and how are we filled with them? (Matt. 5:1-10; 25:37-40; Gal. 5:22-23)

❦ *SAVOR GOD'S TRUTH* ❦

One hot summer day as I was working in the yard, the desperate cries of my neighbor's dog caught my attention. As I rounded the corner, I could see Sneaker tied to a tree in the shade. In his efforts to free himself from the chain that bound him, he had managed to wrap it several times around the tree as well as himself. He was crying loudly because he was unable to move!

When was the last time you felt "chained" to circumstances in your life? What was your response? We cannot always control our circumstances, but we can discover how *not* to let our circumstances control us! The right attitudes and actions in the midst of the circumstance can break the "chains" that bind us.

As we begin our study of Philippians, we find Paul literally in chains, as he is once again under arrest for preaching Christ. Best evidence indicates that Paul is under house arrest in Rome. Though he is continually chained to a Roman soldier (1:13), Paul is not "chained" to his circumstances! His situation could easily lend itself to discouragement, depression, or self-pity. However, we see that Paul's main concern is not himself. Instead, his concern is for his dear Philippian friends whom he had introduced to a personal relationship with Christ.

The Book of Philippians serves, in part, as Paul's thank-you letter to the members of the Philippian church for a gift that they had sent to him by means of Epaphroditus (4:10-19). Yet Paul also wants to encourage these believers, who have become saints through their union with Christ. As Paul wishes them "grace and peace," he is tenderly reminding them of the unmerited favor and the inner tranquility that has been bestowed on them through God the Father and the Lord Jesus Christ.

Paul writes with a servant attitude and a joyful spirit. In fact, joy is clearly the dominant theme of his whole letter. In Philippians 1:1-11, as Paul focuses his thoughts on his beloved Philippians, he bursts into thanksgiving and *joyful prayer!* Could it be that the joy in Paul's life and in his prayer life is the result of his focus on others? I think so!

I have discovered more than once how quickly selfishness can rob me of my joy. The last time was only a few weeks ago. Having been restricted to bed while recovering from foot surgery, I found myself discouraged and somewhat depressed. The surgery had gone well; friends were providing food for my family; my mother-in-law was weekly doing my laundry; and my husband was paying to have the house cleaned. Everything was under control! Everything should have been wonderful, but I felt "chained" to my circumstances. One day while I was reading a Christian book, I realized I was losing my joy. It wasn't my circumstances that were affecting my joy, but it was the way I was responding to them. My thoughts and especially my prayer life had become very self-centered. As I began to focus on others and to concentrate on interceding on their behalf, I felt the fullness of my joy return!

Paul's example not only shows us that *joyful prayer* is *focused on others,* but it is also *fused with sentiment.* Paul feels deep emotions for the Philippians, and he is not shy about sharing his sentiments with them! In Philippians 1:4 Paul states that whenever he prays for the Philippians, it is "always" with joy. Philippians 1:3-11 reflects three sentiments which permit such joyful prayer on their behalf.

First, verses 3-6 reveal that when Paul prays for the Philippians, he prays with *confidence.* His confidence stems from his joyful memories of the Philippians, their partnership (NIV) in the Gospel, and God's faithfulness. How wonderful it is to have only good memories of someone! That is how it is for Paul concerning the Philippians. He is able to thank God every time he remembers them, because of their positive response to the Gospel. Their participation in God's grace had created a special fellowship (KJV) between them. For Paul, this partnership meant not only the joy of sharing a common faith, but also the assurance of knowing that the Philippians were daily participating in the life of God! This assurance rested not on the Philippians, but on God who had transformed their lives by His work of regeneration. Paul's confidence was in the faithfulness of God, who not only initiates salvation but also continues and preserves it until its completion at the glorious coming of Christ.

We, like Paul, need to fuse our prayers with confidence in our great and mighty God! Our confidence needs only rest on the reality of *who* God is. In Ephesians 3:20, we read, "Now to Him who is able to do immeasurably more than all we ask or imagine, according to His power that is at work within us" (NIV).

Second, Philippians 1:7-8 reveals that when Paul prays for the Philippians, he prays with *compassion*. This compassion is a blend of the affections of Paul, the affections of God, and the affections of Christ. We sense that the Philippians are a part of Paul's innermost being, as he states in verse 7, "I have you in my heart." His relationship with them is warm and tender. Just as a loving father feels concern and responsibility for the welfare and growth of his children, Paul feels concern and responsibility for the spiritual growth of the Philippians.

It is the affections of God that allowed Paul and the Philippians to become partakers of His grace (John 3:16; Eph. 2:8-9). As Paul and the Philippians both shared in the gift of God's grace, they also joined their hearts to share a common goal—the furtherance of the Gospel! This goal obviously requires suffering as well as joy. The Philippians have become one with Paul in his persecution through their gifts to him. They are openly identifying themselves with him at a time that is dangerous to do so. They are treating Paul's misfortunes as their own, which magnifies the compassion between them. The warmth of the Philippians' assistance stirs within Paul the pain of separation and causes him to feel an intense longing to be united with them. We find Paul's compassion for the Philippians patterned after that of Christ, as he yearns for them with the affections of Christ.

Paul allowed Christ, who dwelled within him, to love others through him by the power of the Holy Spirit. We too need to be in a vital union with Christ so that we can be used as vessels of love and compassion for others. It is only by loving others with the affections of Christ that we can pray for them effectively. Christlike compassion allows us to identify with others in such a way that their needs become realities to us.

Lastly, in verses 9-11 we see that when Paul prays for the Philippians, he prays with genuine *concern*. Paul's compassion enables him to know how to pray for the Philippians, and in these verses he expresses his concerns specifically.

First, Paul prays that their love will grow in knowledge. According to Paul, real love is not "blind." Real love requires growth and maturation and is based on the principles of God's Word. Love based on knowledge enables a person to love what God "requires" in the way that God "reveals"! Second, Paul prays that the Philippians will be a discerning people. Maturity allows one to discern between good and evil. Paul, however, not only wants them to "perceive" what is morally and ethically superior, but he also prays in his third request that they will "practice" it. He desires the Philippians' actions to be as pure as their love so that their lives will not be offensive to God or to others. Paul is praying for them to be "sincere" as well as "sensitive," since they must one day stand before the Lord and give account of their deeds (2 Cor. 5:10). Last, Paul prays that the lives of the Philippians will show evidences of their right relationship with God. He wants their lives to display the inner qualities described in Galatians 5:22.

Galatians 6:2 says: "Carry each other's burdens, and in this way you will fulfill the law of Christ" (NIV). Are you willing to show that kind of concern? In order to share in someone's joy, you may first have to share in their burdens!

Begin today to "spice up your life with joy" by challenging yourself to a more joyful prayer life! Follow Paul's example and allow your prayers to be focused on others as well as fused with sentiment. Learn to pray for others with confidence, compassion, and concern!

🍂 SEASON YOUR LIFE 🍂

1. Make a list of specific people who give you joy. Spend time each day this week thanking the Lord for them and interceding for their specific needs.

2. Write down specific ways that you can love others with the "affections of Christ." Follow through with at least two of them this week.

3. Make a list of people whose spiritual growth you are concerned about. Using Paul's prayer as a model, pray for them daily.

4. Think about which fruits of righteousness need to increase in your life. What specific actions will you take in order for this to happen?

CHAPTER TWO

Joyful Praise

🔥 SIMMER THESE THOUGHTS 🔥

Read Philippians 1:12-20.

1. What does verse 12 say was the result of Paul's imprisonment? Do you think the outcome was expected or unexpected? Explain why.

2. What was Paul's main concern during his imprisonment? How did Paul use his circumstances for his good and God's glory? (2 Tim. 2:8-9; Acts 28:16-23, 30-31) Do you look for opportunities to make your relationship with Christ known to others?

3. Why did Paul's imprisonment give courage to the brethren? What was the end result? Have you ever been fearful of sharing the Gospel? What could you do to gain courage? (Eph. 6:19-20; 2 Tim. 2:15)

4. In Philippians 1:15-18, compare and contrast the two groups of people who were preaching about Christ while Paul was in prison. Why is Paul not concerned about their different motives? What is his concern? See Galatians 1:6-9.

5. Have you ever questioned the motives of someone who was preaching a true Gospel message? What were your attitudes toward this person? What can you learn from Paul's example?

6. Do you personally share Paul's joy in Philippians 1:18? What could you do to become more excited about the Gospel message and more burdened for those who are spiritually lost?

7. On what two kinds of assistance was Paul depending? In the midst of difficult circumstances, do you seek help from the same resources as Paul? What does Paul expect to gain through this combined assistance? Explain.

8. According to verse 20, what is Paul's utmost desire? How was Christ being exalted in Paul's body in his life? How could Christ be exalted in Paul's death? (1 Cor. 6:19-20; Rom. 12:1-2)

9. What is your utmost desire? How can Christ be exalted in your body through your life or death? (Rom. 14:7-8)

10. List the various attitudes that Paul displays in Philippians 1:12-20. Which attitudes of Paul could help you more effectively live your life? How can we increase the development of godly attitudes and responses in our individual lives?

11. In what way is Paul's life a challenge to you?

✎ SAVOR GOD'S TRUTH ✎

Tears rolled freely down my cheeks as the full impact of her words hit my heart! "Many of you may not know me, but you probably knew my daughter, Missy. You were faithful in praying for her during her battle with cancer. Because of her death and because of the people in this church, I came to know Jesus Christ as my personal Saviour. I just want to praise God tonight!"

This was the testimony of Vi Nix before she was baptized in our Sunday evening service. Her words have been replayed in my mind many times since that night. Her testimony is such a concrete example of how any circumstances in our lives can render themselves worthy of praise if they are used for the advancement of the Gospel! This truth is the theme of what Paul is saying in Philippians 1:12-20.

We find Paul bubbling with *joyous praise* as he proclaims to his Philippian friends the exciting but perhaps unexpected news that his imprisonment is serving to advance the Gospel! One might expect that Paul's confinement would be an obstacle rather than a catalyst for the spreading of the Gospel message. However, we see Paul's situation being advantageous to the Gospel in two ways.

First, *Paul's "chains" have become a "cable of communication"* through which Christ is being preached! Paul is imprisoned like a criminal, but the Word of God is not! Paul is using his chains as an opportunity to share Christ with every prison guard assigned to him as well as anyone else who comes to his quarters. As a result, Paul is able to communicate the Gospel to both Jews (Acts 28:17) and Gentiles (Phile. 10). Therefore, circumstances that could cause frustration and despair instead cause increased joy in Paul!

For many years I was chained to a poor self-image, stemming from the fact that I developed a severe curvature of the spine in fifth grade. At that time, a surgical procedure was not available. By the time it was, my condition allowed for only minimum correction to be obtained. In those sensitive and formative years of junior high and high school, I went through two surgeries, weeks of convalescence in bed, and months in body casts, only to find myself still with a physical deformity that requires hours of shopping to camouflage!

When I came to know Jesus as my personal Saviour, He began to heal my poor self-image through His Word, a process which took years. Finally, I reached the point where I was ready to take everything that He had done in my life in this area and put it into a nine-week, one-hour workshop format to help others. Up to this point, even though I had learned to love myself exactly as I am, I could not say that I felt any "joy" as a result of all that I had been through. But in that first workshop, when someone accepted Jesus as her Saviour because of my testimony, joy exploded within me! I knew at that moment that all my physical and mental pain and suffering counted as nothing in comparison to the value of one soul being added to the kingdom of heaven!

As we continue in this passage of Philippians, we see that Paul's chains have not only become a cable of communication for himself but also for the Christians in Rome. Paul's attitude toward his chains has not only given power to his witness for Christ, but also has given courage to other Christians to actively communicate Christ. Paul's fortitude as a prisoner has enabled them to lay aside their fears and become bolder witnesses themselves. These results have added to Paul's joy, even though he knows that some of the brethren are preaching Christ from motives of envy and rivalry. Galatians 1:8 makes it clear that Paul has no tolerance for anyone who does not preach an accurate and true Gospel.

Therefore, we know that Paul finds no fault with the message of these opposing preachers, only their motives! He realizes that they are trying to promote themselves at his expense, hoping to add to his suffering by their success. Their plans, however, are of no avail whatsoever, because Paul's utmost concern continues to be the proclamation of the Gospel rather than the settling of personal grievances. Paul's praises go to the brethren who preach Christ out of goodwill. These brethren recognize God's divine plan for the ministry of Paul and are determined, because of their love for him, to do their part in carrying out his sole ambition.

We have seen that Paul's chains served not only as an effective line of communication, but that they were also used in Paul's life as a "call" to joy. Both his captivity, as well as the conflict of loyalties among the preachers, served to evoke joy from Paul! This we see in Philippians 1:18a, as he summarizes his reaction to the situation: "But what does it matter? The important thing is that in every way, whether from false motives or true, Christ is preached. And because of this I rejoice" (NIV).

Second, we find Paul turning his imprisonment to the advantage of the spreading of the Gospel because *he uses his "circumstances" as a "platform for praise"!* Paul's example challenges us to make even the worst circumstances in our lives a stage on which we stand to praise God for His divine faithfulness. In verse 18b we see Paul continuing to rejoice as he uses his circumstances as an opportunity to make a profession of confidence and courage based on his faith in the Lord Jesus Christ.

Paul can praise the Lord in the midst of circumstances over which he has no control because he has the assurance that God is in complete control! His faith allows him to "eagerly" anticipate his "unknown" future, as he expresses unwavering confidence in two things.

First, Paul fully expects his circumstances to end in his deliverance. Paul cannot be sure that this deliverance includes his release from prison, but he is confident that this deliverance will be a spiritual victory for him—a victory that includes both his personal salvation as well as his vindication in court. Paul has the well-founded hope of standing unashamed before both his human and his divine Judge!

Second, Paul fully expects Christ to be exalted in his life or in his death. Paul is not concerned with his fate, but rather his overriding concern is that Christ be honored. He is confident that the Gospel will also be vindicated whether it be through his release or his martyrdom. If released, Paul will continue to glorify Christ through his ministry as an apostle; if he is not released, he will glorify Christ by his faithful witness unto death.

Paul realizes that in order for his expectations to be fulfilled, he must rely on the prayers of his Philippian friends as well as the help of the Holy Spirit. Because he is confident that he can depend on these two resources, he is able to be filled with *joyous praise,* rather than fear and despair. He trusts that this human and divine assistance will work together to strengthen him with the boldness and courage he needs to be all that he can be for Christ.

Paul's example is a vivid reminder to us that we too need to daily depend on prayer and the power of the Holy Spirit so that we can be all that God wants us to be! It is so easy to make the mistake of trying to live our lives in our own efforts and self-sufficiency. In Paul we see the truth of 2 Corinthians 3:4-5 which reads, "Such confidence as this is ours through Christ before God. Not that we are competent to claim anything for ourselves, but our competence comes from God" (NIV). Neither our confidence, our competence, nor the claim to any results belongs to us—it all belongs to God!

Do you want to turn a particular circumstance in your life into a cable of communication for Christ? Do you want this circumstance to become a platform for praise? Then make sure that you, like Paul, are divinely equipped!

❧ SEASON YOUR LIFE ❧

1. Reflect on a circumstance in your life to which you feel chained. Pray and ask God how you can begin to use this circumstance as an opportunity to share Christ.

Prayerfully evaluate what your attitudes have been toward this situation. Write down specific ways that you will apply Paul's attitudes to your circumstances. Check your progress in a week.

Read Romans 5:1-5; James 1:1-5; 1 Peter 1:6-9; 5:6-10. Spend time in prayer, praising the Lord!

2. Put into writing how you would share with someone the Gospel message of Jesus Christ (1 Cor. 15:1-6), using the following Scriptures: Romans 3:23; 5:8; 6:23; John 1:12; 3:16; 10:10; 14:6; 1 Corinthians 15:3-6; 2 Corinthians 5:17, 19; Ephesians 1:13-14; 2:8-9; 1 Peter 1:23; 2:2; 1 John 5:11-13; and Revelation 3:20.

Have *you* accepted Christ as your personal Saviour? If not, please do so today by praying this simple prayer of faith:

Dear Heavenly Father,

I realize that I am a sinner. Thank You for sending Jesus to die on the cross for my sins. Please come into my heart and life as my Saviour and my Lord. I give You complete control of my life. Make me into the person You want me to be. Thank You.

In Jesus' Name, Amen.

Spend time praising God for His beautiful plan of salvation!

3. Ask someone to begin praying specifically for you and your effectiveness as a witness for Jesus Christ. Who needs your prayers in this area? Ask the Lord to burden your heart for those around you who do not know Christ. Ask the Lord for opportunities to share His Gospel. Spend time praising the Lord for all those who are faithful in proclaiming the Gospel.

4. Complete the following sentence: This week I will exalt Christ in my body by _____ .

CHAPTER THREE

Joyful Purpose

♠ SIMMER THESE THOUGHTS ♠

Read Philippians 1:21-26.
1. What is Paul's purpose for life as stated in verse 21? Is this your purpose for life? Why or why not? *CHRIST. YES BECAUSE TO SERVE CHRIST, WHO DIED FOR OUR SINS, MEANS ETERNAL LIFE.*

2. Explain "For me to live is Christ" in light of Galatians 2:20 and Colossians 3:1-4. *IF WE FOLLOW CHRIST'S TEACHINGS, NOT ONLY WILL WE KNOW JOY ON THIS EARTH, BUT WE WILL ALSO HAVE ETERNAL JOY & LIFE AFTER DEATH.*

3. Read the following passages, and then summarize why death is a "gain" for a believer in Christ: 2 Corinthians 5:1, 6, 8; John 5:24; 11:25-26; 14:1-4. Do you share Paul's optimistic feelings concerning death? Why or why not? *YES, DEATH IS NOT TO BE FEARED RATHER A TIME TO REJOICE FOR WE WILL BE WITH OUR MAKER FOREVER.*

4. What inner struggle does Paul face in Philippians 1:21-26? What are Paul's desires? What are his decisions? *PAUL WANTS TO BE WITH CHRIST IN HEAVEN BUT DOESN'T WANT TO LEAVE THE PEOPLE BECAUSE THEY STILL NEED HIM TO SHOW THEM THE PATH TO CHRIST.*

25

5. What does Paul mean by "fruitful labor" in verse 22? What actions will this fruitful labor include? (See John 4:35b-36; 15:16; Colossians 1:10; and Romans 1:13.) How can you become more fruitful in your labor for the Lord? (2 Peter 1:5-10; John 15:1-8)

1. BRINGING CHRIST'S FLOCK HOME,
2. ACTIONS: SPEAKING THE GOSPEL AT EVERY OPPORTUNITY.
3. BRING GOODNESS, KNOWLEDGE, SELF-CONTROL, PERSEVERANCE, GODLINESS, BROTHERLY KINDNESS, LOVE INTO OUR LIVES.

6. What actions cause a person to "progress" in his faith? How are "progress" in the faith and "joy" in the faith related? Evaluate your own progress and joy.

1. SAME AS ABOVE
2. TO PROGRESS IN ONE'S FAITH BRINGS ETERNAL JOY.

Read Philippians 1:27-30.

7. Read the following Scriptures, and fill in the chart concerning what *actions* and *attitudes* are involved in conducting "yourselves in a manner worthy of the Gospel."

	actions	attitudes
Colossians 1:9-12	PRAYER	SPIRITUAL KNOWLEDGE ENDURANCE PATIENCE
Colossians 3:12-17	CLOTHE YOURSELF	COMPASSION KINDNESS HUMILITY GENTLENESS PATIENCE
Ephesians 4:13	UNITY IN FAITH	
2 Peter 1:4-10	SEE 5,3	EFFECTIVE PRODUCTIVE

8. What does Philippians 1:27b say that the Philippians' purpose in life will be as a result of conducting themselves in a manner worthy of the Gospel? Are you motivated toward this same purpose in your life? Why or why not?

THEY WILL STAND FIRM IN ONE SPIRIT.

9. What is the "sign" in verse 28 that Paul is talking about? How is this sign a reflection of salvation and destruction? (2 Thes. 1:4-8; Col. 1:23) BEING FRIGHTENED

10. What two privileges are ours as Christians? In what ways did Paul suffer for Christ according to 2 Corinthians 11:23-28? How do Christians suffer for Christ today? How can the following verses help us to adopt Paul's attitude toward suffering: Matthew 5:10-12; 1 Peter 4:12-16?

BELIEVING & SUFFERING

2. BEATEN, FLOGGED, STONED, SHIPWRECKED, LABORED & TOILED, WENT w/o SLEEP, WENT HUNGRY, WAS COLD & NAKED

❧ *SAVOR GOD'S TRUTH* ❧

Jelly beans in the microwave? Let me explain. I had made a decision to go on a diet and lose my five familiar pounds. I refer to them as familiar because I have lost and gained those same five pounds more times than I care to think about! Before I made my diet decision, I had given in to the tempting Easter displays and bought a bag of jelly beans—for my kids, of course! (The fact that jelly beans happen to be one of my weaknesses only influenced me slightly.) After eating all the black ones out of the package the night before my diet began, I put the jelly beans in the freezer. Frozen Snickers bars are wonderful, but frozen jelly beans are not! They become hard as rocks and are impossible to eat without serious tooth damage. How do I know? I am experienced at this type of thing! After two weeks of faithful dieting, my desires became stronger than my decision!

One afternoon while I was home studying, I decided I would reward myself with just a handful of jelly beans. Not wanting to wait for them to thaw, I experimented with them—one at a time—in the microwave. The first one blew up; the second one melted; but the third one was just right! After mastering the time and temperature, I was able to eat a handful—well, two large handfuls of jelly beans, and then go back to studying. But you know, giving in to my desires was not nearly as rewarding as I thought it would be. My happiness was short-lived, since my desires cost me a pound! Living by my decision would have been much more rewarding!

Paul deals with this issue of *desires and decisions* in Philippians 1:21-30. In verses 21-26 Paul discusses his own desires and decisions. As he does, we see him as an example of someone who is constantly able to put aside his own desires in order to accomplish the joyful purpose of living decisively for Christ. However, we also see that Paul's decision to live for Christ is inevitably a decision to live for others. In verses 27-30 we see Paul exhorting the Philippians concerning their desires and decisions, so that they might grab hold of his joyful purpose for life.

Christ is the very essence of Paul's life! Paul is so totally committed to Christ that Christ is not only Paul's reason for living but also Paul's reason for dying. We see in verses 21-26 that life and death hold equal attraction for Paul. So much so, that as he thinks about these two alternatives that face him, he finds himself in a dilemma, torn by two equally competitive consequences. Remaining alive means that Paul can continue to do what he loves to do—labor for the cause of Christ by preaching the Gospel, establishing churches, and discipling believers. Dying, however, is also an opportunity for Paul. His martyrdom will not only honor Christ and add witness to the Gospel, but his death will also bring his reward of being in eternal fellowship with Christ. As Paul thinks of the joy of being in the presence of the Lord, intense emotion causes him to suddenly express his inner desires, as he states in verse 23b, "I desire to depart and be with Christ, which is better by far" (NIV). Fruitful labor for the cause of Christ was not easy labor. Paul was constantly met with opposition and physical hardship (2 Cor.1:23-28). In this sense, it would be an advantage for Paul to leave this world and live with Christ.

However, Paul is not concerned with what is advantageous for himself. His main concern, as always, is for Christ's work and the needs of his fellow believers. Immediately after he expresses his personal desires, Paul puts them aside by focusing his attention on his pastoral responsibilities. In Philippians 1:24 he states, "But it is more necessary for you that I remain in the body" (NIV).

Considering all factors, Paul concludes that it is likely that he will remain in order to serve the saints. He realizes that his release would be a source of joy and encouragement for the Philippians since they have prayed faithfully for his deliverance. However, Paul also knows that he is needed to instruct them in spiritual truths. By being with them again, Paul would be able to increase their maturity in Christ and, as a result, deepen their joy in their Christian faith.

Though Paul is giving serious thought to his future, he does not have the prerogative of choosing his fate. Since he expresses such indecisiveness in these verses, we can assume that he is glad he does not have that right. Paul's faith allows him to rest in the fact that the Lord is in complete control, and that He will make the best choice for him.

Paul's example teaches us a valuable lesson! We learn from Paul that our spiritual desires must be in subjection to God's will as much as our physical desires. Paul is completely willing to replace his own desires with God's decisions! What about you? Are you willing to submit all your desires—both physical and spiritual—to God? Are you willing to replace your desires with His decisions for your life?

In verses 27-30 Paul confronts the Philippians in regard to their desires and decisions. He challenges them to make two decisions concerning their actions. First, he exhorts them to *serve Christ by conducting themselves in a manner worthy of the Gospel.* As citizens of the kingdom of heaven (Eph. 2:19), Paul challenges them to reflect the highest standards of behavior in their relationships among themselves, as well as with the outside world. As the Philippians decisively live for Christ in this worthy manner, Paul expects three results. First, he expects the Philippians to stand firm in one spirit. This involves putting aside any individual desires that would lead to dissension. They must, through the power of the Holy Spirit, achieve internal harmony so that they present a steadfast front to the outside world. This unity of thought and action is necessary to bring about the second expected result—that of contending as one man for the faith of the Gospel. Paul expects the Philippian's conduct to enable them to strive together in a unified effort to "fearlessly" promote the Gospel as well as prevail over their adversaries. Though the Philippians are experiencing the pressures of persecution, Paul expects their joint efforts to enable them to solidly resist their enemies with endurance instead of giving in with fear. To suffer for the sake of Christ is the third expected result of deciding to live in a manner worthy of the Gospel. Paul, however, wants the Philippians to concentrate not on this result but instead on their response. Their ability to respond to this persecution with constancy and their resistance to be intimidated is a demonstration of the salvation that is theirs. Their response is also a sign of their enemies' ultimate destruction, as the church continues to prevail regardless of attacks.

The Philippians' decision to worthily serve Christ brings with it the second decision of *sharing in Paul's struggle* (2 Tim. 2:3). Therefore, Paul closes this passage by encouraging them with divine principles concerning suffering. Paul reminds them that suffering for the cause of Christ is as much a part of their joyful purpose for life as is the privilege of believing in Him (Phil. 3:7-10). It may not be their desire, but it is God's decision. After all, His own Son learned obedience through the things which He suffered (Heb. 5:8).

Do you share Paul's joyful purpose for living? If not, perhaps you need to evaluate the extent to which you worthily serve Christ, as well as your attitudes and responses toward suffering. Why not make the decision today to let Christ be your reason for living and, if necessary, your reason for dying? As you replace your desires with His decisions, joy will follow, for in true surrender His decisions become your newly discovered desires!

🍂 *SEASON YOUR LIFE* 🍂

1. Complete the following sentence: For me to live is *CHRIST*. Does your answer align with Paul's, or has something or someone in your life taken Christ's place? What specific changes do you need to make in order to have Christ be your purpose for living?

2. Are you afraid to die? Read and meditate on Hebrews 2:9, 14-15; 1 Corinthians 15:51-57; and 1 John 5:11-13. Jesus came to deliver you from being enslaved to the fear of death. Through Him you can partake of the victory over death. Eternal life is yours when Jesus dwells within you! (See part 2 of the "Season Your Life" section of Chapter 2.)

3. In what area(s) of your life are you living by your desires instead of your decisions? List specific ways that you can concentrate on Christ and others in order to overcome these selfish desires.

4. Are you progressing in your faith? What does 1 Peter 2:2 say is necessary for growth as a Christian? Is reading God's Word a *daily* discipline for you? If not, commit yourself to fifteen minutes of Bible reading each day. Set aside a specific time during your day for your "appointment" with God. Be consistent! Keep a spiritual diary by daily writing down how you can apply what you read to your own life.

5. Evaluate your actions and attitudes according to the chart in question 7 of the "Simmer These Thoughts" section. What can you do to make your manner of life worthier of the Gospel that you represent?

6. Are you suffering from trials or persecution today? For encouragement, read James 1:1-3, 12; 1 Peter 1:6-7; 5:6-10. Memorize the verses that give you the most comfort.

CHAPTER FOUR

❦ *SIMMER THESE THOUGHTS* ❦

Read Philippians 2:1-11. Reread 2:1-4.
1. According to verse 1, what benefits do we obtain from our union in Christ? How can each one promote unity within the body of Christ? (Col. 1:17; 3:12-17; Eph. 4:1-6; 1 Cor. 12:7, 12-27)

1. ENCOURAGEMENT, COMFORT, FELLOWSHIP.

2. THEY ALL PROMOTE LOVE WHICH BINDS THEM TOGETHER IN PERFECT UNITY.

2. Using Philippians 2:2-4, fill in the following chart, in order to explain Paul's instructions for obtaining harmony among the brethren:

Needed Actions	Needed Attitudes	Attitudes/Actions to Avoid
SAME LOVE	*LIKE MINDED ONE IN SPIRIT & PURPOSE HUMILITY*	*SHELFISH AMBITION VAIN CONCEIT*

In what specific ways can we, as Christians, do and have these necessary actions and attitudes toward each other?

WE NEED THE SPIRIT OF GOD WITHIN US.

3. How would you define humility? How does the dictionary define humility? Read Matthew 23:5-12; Luke 22:24-27; John 13:3-5, 12-17; and 1 Peter 5:5-6, and then summarize the biblical perspective of humility. In what ways does humility produce unity?

1. MODEST, NOT A BRAGGER OF ONESELF.
2. UNPRETENTIOUS, LOWLY, MODEST
3. TO FOLLOW CHRIST'S TEACHINGS & SERVE HIM HUMBLY.

4. What correlations are there between unity and joy? How was unity related to joy in Paul's life? How is unity related to joy in your life?

Reread Philippians 2:5-11.

5. According to verses 6-8, in what ways did Christ Jesus show Himself to be the supreme example of humility? How does His example help you to be obedient to Paul's exhortation in verses 3 and 4?

1. HE BECAME A SERVANT TO GOD, CONSIDERING HIMSELF HUMAN, HE DID NOT CONSIDER HIMSELF TO BE EQUAL TO GOD.
2. IF JESUS, IN ALL HIS GLORY, BEING SUPREME TO HUMANS, CAN HUMBLE HIMSELF TO SERVE GOD WE AS HUMANS SHOULD TRY TO FOLLOW CHRIST.

6. Summarize the character qualities that are found in a person who has the attitude or "mind" (kjv) of Christ. Evaluate the degree to which you have the attitude of Christ. What specific things can you do to increase your like-mindedness with Christ?

ENCOURAGEMENT, COMFORT, FELLOWSHIP, TENDERNESS COMPASSION AND MOST OF ALL LOVE.

7. What do verses 6-8 reveal about Jesus' partnership with God and Jesus' partnership with man? How do Isaiah 53:4-6, Hebrews 2:17-18, and Matthew 10:32-33 add to the understanding of this partnership?

THAT EVEN THO JESUS IS THE VERY NATURE OF GOD WHEN HE TOOK HUMAN FORM HE CONSIDERED HIMSELF NOTHING AND BECAME A SERVANT OF GOD.

8. What was God's response to Jesus' humility? Read Matthew 18:4; Luke 14:7-11; 18:9-14; Proverbs 15:33; 22:4. Then explain how

our humble actions will be rewarded. How are these truths an encouragement to you?

OUR HUMBLE ACTIONS WILL ENSURE US A PLACE IN HEAVEN.

9. What two actions are involved in submission to the Lord Jesus? Is this submission, which is described in Philippians 2:10-11, the same as salvation? Why or why not?

BOWING TO JESUS' NAME & CONFESSING THAT JESUS CHRIST IS LORD. YES, FOR IF WE FOLLOW JESUS' TEACHINGS & SERVE THE LORD WITH HUMILITY, WE WILL HAVE ETERNAL LIFE.

10. What actions have you taken to proclaim your partnership with Christ? What actions and attitudes in your life proclaim your partnership with fellow believers?

🍃 *SAVOR GOD'S TRUTH* 🍃

It was not an ordinary wedding! Soon after my husband Joe and I were seated, we realized that the guests were there not only to witness a special union but to worship. Our hearts felt an extraordinary call to celebration! From the beginning to the end, the ceremony was a joyful proclamation of Christian partnership.

Through their choice of songs, Dawn and David first proclaimed their individual partnerships with Christ ("He Has Chosen You for Me" and "I See Jesus in You"). Then they announced the quality of partnership that they have, and will continue to have, with each other as partners in Him ("Friends" and "Household of Faith"). Unity and harmony reigned as we the congregation sang, "Surely the Presence of the Lord Is in This Place" and prayed "The Lord's Prayer." The joy we were feeling for Dawn and David was made complete as we affirmed our partnership as Christians and celebrated together one love and Spirit and purpose. The last song, "O, How He Loves You and Me," directed our thoughts to dwell on the glorious love of God which makes partnership in Christ possible.

As we left the church, Joe and I heard many comments from others which reflected the same uplifted and joyous spirit that had been created within our hearts. We knew why. As Dawn and David experienced the joy of entering into their partnership in marriage, we were blessed with the opportunity of experiencing the joy of our partnership in Christ!

In Philippians 2:1-11, we find Paul exhorting the Philippians concerning Christian partnership. He reminds them that their partnership with Christ is the basis for their partnership with each other. He directs them to blend their minds with Christ's so that they might imitate the humility of Christ. Through this humility, they will achieve unity which will result in harmonious living for them as well as in completed joy for Paul.

Let's look first at Paul's exhortation to the Philippians as *partners with Christ.* Paul wants the Philippians to understand that their partnership with Christ should be both the "motivation" and the "means" for achieving unity among themselves. He points out that in their vital union with Christ, they themselves receive blessings of comfort and encouragement which, in turn, should motivate them to strive for oneness with each other. Paul appeals to the Philippians to allow the constraining power of love, the fellowship of the Spirit, and the qualities of tenderness and compassion to bind them together as members of a family in a household of faith. Paul realizes that struggles and divisions within the church can be as threatening to the Philippians as their struggles with enemies outside of the church. For that reason, he challenges the Philippians to examine their relationships within the church and to resolve any strife or conflict. In light of Paul's admonition in verse 3, it appears that selfishness and conceit were evils that threatened the Christian community at Philippi.

We must be realistic and realize that these same evils threaten our churches today. Too often selfish ambition and vain conceit spoil our fellowship and destroy our Christian witness. Paul's challenge to the Philippians is also a challenge to us. Examine the spiritual heartbeat of the relationships in your church. Are there symptoms of heart problems? Do *you* have a healthy heart?

Paul offers an antidote for these diseases of the heart—humility. He also offers a supreme example of this humility in verses 5-8—Christ Himself. When Paul states in verse 5, "Your attitude should be the same as that of Christ Jesus" (NIV), he indicates to the Philippians that their partnership with Christ provides the means of cultivating the humility essential for their unity. Only through their union with Christ can they be transformed into His likeness (2 Cor. 3:18). As Christ increases in their lives, and the Philippians' self-importance decreases (see John 3:30), they will be better able to imitate the humility of Christ. In verses 6-8, we see Christ willingly giving up what was His by right and joyfully accepting the consequences of self-denial. Though He did not lay aside His divine attributes, He did lay aside their use. He, who possessed the very nature of God, stripped Himself of all privileges and rightful dignity in order to take on the very nature of a servant. By sharing man's appearance and weaknesses, He, who was the very likeness of God, humbled Himself to be made into the likeness of man. Then He humbled Himself further by climaxing His life of sacrifice with the most disgraceful of all deaths—death on a cross. He, who could have seized or demanded honor, chose instead to earn honor.

Christ reflects the attitude of mind that we should have in our personal relationships. True humility goes beyond the dictionary's definition of meekness and modesty. True humility involves self-denial and servanthood. How does your humility compare with Christ's? What "rights" are you clinging to that are keeping you from a life of servanthood? Is the emphasis of your life sacrifice or self?

Second, let's look at Paul's exhortation to the Philippians as *partners with each other*. Paul admonishes them to be in one accord, sharing a common purpose and showing each other mutual love and respect. This like-mindedness would enable them to give preference and consideration to one another over themselves. Paul is challenging them to a broader outlook in which being concerned with the needs and interests of others replaces the selfishness of only caring for oneself. Paul wants the Philippians to take the humility resulting from their partnership with Christ and *apply it to their partnership with each other!* The result will be a climate where harmony and joy can flourish.

As I have studied this passage of humility expressed in servanthood, my mind has many times been drawn to my memories of LaVon Meek. LaVon was a dear friend and neighbor who went to be with the Lord in March 1987 after a lengthy battle with cancer. Her entire life was devoted to meeting the needs of her large family (six children and fourteen grandchildren) and her many friends. "Self" was never an issue for LaVon as she daily served others. When my daughter Shannon was born, LaVon gave a shower for me, ran errands for me, and organized meals for my family for a full week! While I was in the hospital, she helped Joe with the laundry, the house, and my son Shawn.

Even as she lay dying, she found ways to look out for the interests of those she loved. Consider these acts of a suffering woman in severe pain: She provided engraved Bibles for her children to be delivered on their birthdays; she gave each grandchild a framed picture of Jesus with a handwritten, personal note on the back, accompanied by a unique, glow-in-the-dark, bedtime prayer; she spent quality time with each family member to say a special good-bye and make sure they were right with the Lord; she exhorted others with cards and phone calls until she could no longer write or talk; and she made sure that, when she was no longer able, her personal funds continued to be distributed all over the country for the furtherance of the Gospel and the support of God's workers. LaVon was able to maintain her joy, even to the tragic end of her earthly life, because of her partnership with Christ and her partnership with others. LaVon will long be remembered by many, for while she was living and while she was dying, she deeply impacted the lives of others!

Paul closes this passage by describing God's response to Christ's humility. In Philippians 2:9-11, God proclaims His partnership with Christ by exalting Christ in position and title. Paul intends for this example of exaltation to encourage the Philippians by showing them the victory that follows a life of humility. Paul wants them to grasp the certainty of the hope that is theirs—that is, that God will one day proclaim His partnership with them if they proclaim their partnership with Christ. However, since everyone everywhere will eventually confess Christ as Lord, the issue of partnership becomes a matter of the heart and the hands of time. In order for this confession to result in *a partnership in joy*, it must come from a heart under the possession of Christ, and it must take place in this lifetime.

Have you entered into this partnership of joy? Have you humbled yourself before God so that you might humble yourself before man? May your joy, like Paul's, be made complete as you experience unity with God and harmony with man!

❧ SEASON YOUR LIFE ❧

1. Evaluate your actions and attitudes according to the chart in question 2 of "Simmer These Thoughts." Ask God to show you your weaknesses and convict you of any wrong attitudes or actions. Confess your failures and shortcomings and receive His forgiveness (1 John 1:9). Spend time in prayer, seeking His help in your areas of inadequacy (2 Cor. 3:5).

2. Commit yourself to being a "servant" this week. Pray each morning for God to alert you to the interests and needs of others and to show you ways you can serve them. Consider what sacrifices you might have to make in order to be obedient to God's promptings. At the end of each day, evaluate whether you primarily served self or others.

3. Make a list of actions you will take to promote unity in your family, at work, in your neighborhood, and at church. Follow through with your ideas. Praise the Lord as you experience the end results.

4. Meditate on Christ's obedience, submission, and humility in Philippians 2:6-8. What changes need to be made in your life in order to adopt Christ's attitudes in these areas?

5. Fill in the following blank: This week I will display the attitude of Christ by _____.

6. Take time to bow your knees before Jesus. Worship and adore Him. Delight yourself in the joy of Him as Saviour and Lord!

CHAPTER FIVE

❧ SIMMER THESE THOUGHTS ❧

Read Philippians 3:17-19, then 3:1-3.
1. Why could Paul feel confident in commanding others to follow his example? (1 Cor. 11:1) What makes this confidence different from spiritual pride?

   1. BECAUSE HE WAS FOLLOWING THE EXAMPLE OF CHRIST.

   2.

2. According to Galatians 5:16-21, describe those who are considered to be "enemies of the Cross." How else does Paul describe them in Philippians 3:2? What canine characteristics might they possess to earn them such a title?

   1. THOSE WHO ACTS OF SINFUL NATURE ARE SEXUAL IMMORALITY, IMPURITY & DEBAUCHERY, IDOLATRY & WITCHCRAFT, HATRED, DISCORD, JEALOUSY, FITS OF RAGE, SELFISH AMBITION, DISSENSIONS, FACTIONS & ENVY, DRUNKENNESS, ORGIES.
   2. AS DOGS, MEN WHO DO EVIL, MUTILATORS OF THE FLESH.

3. Explain in your own words the destiny, the desires, the goals, and the glory of the enemies of the Cross, as stated in Philippians 3:19. See 2 Peter 2:1-19 for additional insight.

   THEIR DESTINY IS ~~IS~~ DESTRUCTION ~~RIGHTEOUS~~ THEIR GOALS STOMACH, SATISFY DESIRES, GLORY IS THEIR SHAME.

41

Read Philippians 2:12-18.
4. According to Ephesians 2:8-9, how is one saved? With that answer in mind, explain "work out your salvation" in relation to the following verses: 1 Peter 2:2-3; Ephesians 4:11-15; 1 Timothy 4:6-12; and Hebrews 5:11-14.

ONE IS SAVED BY GRACE, THRU FAITH.

5. According to Philippians 2:12-13, explain in your own words the correlation between the work we do and the work God does. What should be our attitude as we work out our salvation? How do you understand this attitude? (Heb. 12:28-29; Eph. 6:5; 2 Cor. 7:1)

6. What are the causes and the results of grumbling and arguing? How do these practices keep us from being the blameless children of God that Paul exhorts us to be? How do these practices affect our joy?

7. What is the Word of Life? (See John 6:68-69; 1 John 1:1-4; and Hebrews 4:12.) According to Philippians 2:15-16, what is our responsibility concerning this Word of Life? Explain what it means to "shine as stars" in relation to Matthew 5:14-16; John 8:12; 1 Thessalonians 5:5; Ephesians 5:8; and 2 Corinthians 4:6.

8. What pattern for joy does Paul give his readers in Philippians 2:17-18? How can you apply this to your life?

Read Philippians 2:19-24.

9. Why did Paul "prefer" to send Timothy to the Philippians? How was Timothy following the pattern set by Paul in 2:2-4? In what ways had Timothy "proven" himself?

10. Do Christian leaders need to prove themselves today? Why or why not? As a representative of Christ, are you "preferred" and "proven"?

Read Philippians 2:25-30.

11. What titles does Paul use to describe Epaphroditus? In what ways did Epaphroditus fulfill these roles of Christian partnership? How can we be "soldiers" of Jesus Christ today? (2 Tim. 2:3-4; Eph. 6:10-18)

12. What did Paul do in Philippians 2:25-30 to promote joy among the brethren? What can we do to encourage joyful relationships among the people we know? What pattern of behavior does Paul feel is worthy of honor?

🍂 SAVOR GOD'S TRUTH 🍂

An industrious mother of a child in my daughter's room at school decided to make a "memory quilt" for the teacher. Each child in the room was to decorate a square of cloth by doing needlework or by using one of the many permanent craft paints which are available. When Shannon and I went to the craft store to choose the medium that she would use for her square, we were intrigued by the large variety of craft displays. Above all of the craft supplies were examples showing what the finished product would look like, depending on what method was chosen. The beauty of the examples made them all enticing, but Shannon finally chose one that she liked best and wanted to copy. We bought the supplies that were needed to exactly reproduce her favorite display onto her square.

I was feeling a little inadequate at the task ahead and thought I should warn Shannon that, while we would do our best, ours may not look quite as nice as the example she had seen. Her enthusiasm and confidence, however, quickly dispelled any thoughts of inadequacy, as she said, "Aw, don't worry, Mom. It'll turn out great! All we have to do is read the directions and follow the pattern!"

In Philippians 3:17, Paul says, "Join with others in following my example, brothers, and take note of those who live according to the pattern we gave you" (NIV). Paul is challenging the Philippians, as well as us, to imitate examples of godliness. Paul feels competent in commanding others to follow his example because he knows that he is patterning his life after Christ (1 Cor. 11:1).

However, the pronoun "we" in verse 17 points out to the Philippians that Paul is not to be their only role model. Paul is saying that there are others who have also patterned their lives after Christ, and he wants the Philippians to pay attention to the high standards of conduct of these godly men. In verse 17, Paul is literally saying, "You have us as a pattern." He is including Timothy and Epaphroditus as examples along with himself. It is important to realize that Paul is not telling the Philippians to pattern themselves after man, but rather to imitate the pattern of God found in man! Paul's main concern was always to motivate believers toward Christlikeness.

Philippians 2:12–3:3 and 3:17-19 considers the examples of Paul, Timothy, and Epaphroditus and the patterns for Christian living that they put forth by modeling. Paul presents a *Pattern of Contrast;* Timothy, a *Pattern of Character;* and Epaphroditus, a *Pattern of Companionship.*

Paul's pattern is found in Philippians 2:12-18; 3:1-3; and 3:18-19. He paints a vivid picture of the differences between the children of God and the enemies of the Cross. He dramatically presents the Philippians with a pattern for living by the use of contrast in the areas of destiny, desires, goals, and glory.

Paul first points out that the enemies of the Cross, whom he reproachfully refers to as "dogs," are doomed for eternal misery. These opponents of God's truth were known to "dog" the footsteps of Paul, attacking the vulnerable with false doctrines. As evil workers, they succumb to Satan's power and they "work out" their destruction through evil deeds.

In contrast, the destiny of the children of God, whom Paul lovingly refers to as "brothers," will be eternal life through their salvation in Jesus Christ. Paul exhorts the Philippians to continue to "work out" this salvation through spiritual growth and development. Their salvation was a free gift. They did not have to "work for" it, but they are expected to "work at" it, and they are to do so with an attitude of reverence and due respect. Paul is reminding them that the acceptance of this gift brings with it certain obligations—one of which is obedience.

After one displays initial obedience by receiving the Gospel, he is expected to express continuing obedience by pursuing progress in his Christian life. Paul's encouragement lies in the fact that it is God Himself "working in" the believer that allows him to carry out such a task!

When my son Shawn was two years old, a friend of mine gave him a small car that she bought at a garage sale. Anything with wheels always received Shawn's full attention. He spent many hours playing with his new toy. Sometime later, he came running to show me a compartment that he had found inside the car. None of us had realized it, but the car could be battery-operated. Shawn had been delighted with his gift before, but his joy was made full as we placed a battery inside, and he discovered the power that was made available whenever he turned on the small switch under the car!

In the believer's life, God works like a battery. By working through His Holy Spirit within us, He enables us to make our salvation operational. He energizes our wills and produces within us the desire to live righteously. In addition, He then gives us the power and energy to obediently follow through with our intentions. It is up to us, however, to activate this energy and power. How? We can "turn on the switch" through such activities or disciplines as Bible reading and prayer. What else can you think of that can help you start your engine? Are you running on manpower or God's power? Perhaps it is time to change your battery!

The second contrast which Paul uses to portray his pattern for living concerns life's desires. Paul reveals that the enemies of the Cross live very self-centered lives in which their own appetites and desires come first. The child of God, however, is called to live a Christ-centered life in which he sacrificially serves others as an outpouring of his faith. These labors are the basis of Paul's *Pattern for Joy* which he invites the Philippians to copy (Phil. 2:17-18). Paul depicts the joy that one finds whenever he plants, nourishes, or, if necessary, gives up his life for another's faith. Paul is an example of one who joyfully sacrifices himself for others, whether it be in life or death. Paul saves his tears for the souls of others (Phil. 3:18), rather than using them on himself and his suffering. Paul's desire is for the Philippians to imitate these attitudes and actions which spring forth from his heart.

The third contrast of Paul's pattern involves the goals of life. He challenges the children of God to present themselves without fault or blame, in comparison to the enemies of the Cross who, as a part of a depraved society, are content to be corrupt. By making it their objective to maintain a character and conduct free of criticism, the children of God can be used as vessels through which the light of the world (John 8:12) can shine forth to those who live in moral darkness. They can fulfill their responsibility of witnessing by allowing their influence as children of light (1 Thes. 5:5) to dispel the darkness of unbelief. While the enemies of the Cross remain earthly minded, fixing their attention on physical and material interests, the children of God concentrate on being heavenly minded by firmly holding fast to the truth of the Gospel in order to successfully hold it forth to the world.

Last, Paul addresses the issue of glory in these two groups of people. The enemies of the Cross exalt themselves, putting confidence in the efforts of their own flesh, while the children of God glory in the Saviour, putting all their confidence in the Spirit. In contrast to an enemy of the Cross, the child of God learns to disregard pride and find full satisfaction in the hope made available by Christ alone. He distrusts self, realizing the danger of a soul living independently from Christ. His approval and acceptance is the result of the grace of God, instead of his own efforts.

Does Paul's pattern of contrast reveal any opposing behaviors in your life? Are you patterning yourself after a child of God or an enemy of the Cross? Do you know your destiny? What are your desires and goals? Do you exalt yourself or God?

The example of Timothy, as seen in Philippians 2:19-24, reveals a *Pattern of Character.* Paul presents Timothy to the Philippians as one who is "preferred" and "proven" because of Timothy's character qualities. First, he is preferred because of his kindred spirit with Paul. Paul wants the Philippians to realize that Timothy is as genuinely concerned for their welfare and as devoted to their interests as he is. In this respect, Timothy proves himself to be a living, breathing example of Paul's teachings, as he imitates the humility of Christ (Phil. 2:3-8). He also proves his character by his reputation and his relationship with Paul. The Philippians had witnessed, over the years, Timothy's faithful service with Paul for the advancement of the Gospel. They viewed him as a man of God, working in close association with Paul as Paul's true child in the faith (1 Tim. 1:2).

As a representative of Jesus Christ, are you preferred and proven? In what further ways do you need to pattern your character after Timothy's?

In the example of Epaphroditus (Phil. 2:25-30), we see a *Pattern of Companionship.* Paul strongly commends Epaphroditus to the Philippians as his fellow believer, fellow worker, fellow soldier, and fellow servant. Paul places great value in the elements of companionship that he and Epaphroditus had shared, and he wants to make sure that the Philippians receive him with joy and honor.

As a sharer of spiritual life with Paul, Epaphroditus willingly participated in the labors, as well as the dangers, involved in proclaiming the Gospel. Epaphroditus also shared with Paul the common bond of servanthood expressed in sacrificial service for the benefit of others. Paul praises the way in which Epaphroditus served him as a messenger and a minister. Epaphroditus not only brought Paul the Philippians' gift (4:18), but he also stayed and ministered to his needs under hazardous circumstances. Paul affirms that Epaphroditus risked his life in order to do for him what the Philippians could not do.

What are you doing to share in the ministry of the Gospel of Christ? Where can you help carry the load that another saint is carrying alone? What patterns of companionship, seen in the example of Epaphroditus, do you need to imitate?

As we have contemplated the examples of these three men of God and have traced their individual patterns, we have discovered a common *Pattern for Joy.* This pattern was revealed in the life of Paul and exemplified by the lives of Timothy and Epaphroditus. All three regarded their own lives as sacrifices, presented to God through faithful, selfless service, as a result of faith, and for the spiritual benefit of others. Are you ready to imitate this pattern of joy? If you are a child of God, preferred and proven, working out your salvation as a companion of the Gospel, Paul promises you a "carbon copy" of his joy!

🦋 *SEASON YOUR LIFE* 🦋

1. Who in your life has provided you with a pattern for Christian living? In what specific ways has the example of this person(s) drawn you closer to God? Spend time in prayer praising God for this positive influence(s) on your life. Take time to write a note of appreciation to this person(s), expressing your thankfulness for the way God has used him/her in your life.

2. Read 1 Corinthians 4:16. Do you feel confident in urging others to imitate you in your Christian walk? Why or why not? Do you suppose there are those who imitate you without an invitation? Reflect on whom this might be. How can you improve the pattern for Christian living that others copy from you? Does your pattern, like Paul's, include joy? Spend time in prayer asking God to help you become a more Christlike example for others.

3. How would you evaluate your spiritual progress? In what ways are you working out your salvation in spiritual growth and development? In what areas are you spiritually immature? What can you do to become more mature? Ask God to guide you in "growing up" in the full knowledge of Him. Prayerfully consider steps you can take to keep your mind set on things above.

4. In a notebook, keep track for one week of every time that you find yourself complaining or arguing. Evaluate your performance. Do the results surprise you? Is there need for improvement? If you have been guilty of these behaviors, confess them as sin and joyfully receive God's forgiveness.

5. List three specific ways that you will shine forth as light this week in a dark world. Ask God's help in doing it!

6. In what ways do you need to become more like Timothy? Like Epaphroditus? What specific things can you do this week to imitate their attitudes and/or actions toward others?

CHAPTER SIX

♣ *SIMMER THESE THOUGHTS* ♣

Read Philippians 3:4-16, 20-21.

1. In order to better understand Paul's joyful pursuit in this third chapter of Philippians, read about his conversion in Acts 9:1-32. By what name was Paul first known? (Acts 13:9)

SAUL

Reread Philippians 3:4-9.

2. In what Jewish qualifications did Paul put his confidence before he came to know Jesus as his Saviour? How did these "advantages" become "disadvantages" for Paul? Contrast the pursuits of Paul before and after his conversion.

1. HE WAS A PHARISEE BY LAW, HIS ZEAL WAS IN PERSECUTING THE CHURCH & HIS LEGALISTIC RIGHTEOUSNESS WAS FAULTLESS.

2. BECAUSE HIS FORMER "ADVANTAGES" IS REPRESENTATIVE OF ALL SINNERS.

3. Explain Paul's losses and gains in Philippians 3:7-9 in relation to Luke 9:23-25. What are the differences between "legalistic" righteousness and the righteousness of God? (Rom. 3:20-23; 9:30-32; 10:9-10; 2 Cor. 5:21) Evaluate your own pursuit of righteousness.

1. YOU HAVE TO LOSE YOUR OLD WAYS OF SELF CENTEREDNESS OR EARTHLY GAINS TO GAIN EVERLASTING LIFE WITH JESUS BY FOLLOWING HIS FOOTSTEPS.

2. LEGALISTIC RIGHTEOUSNESS IS UPHOLDING LAWS THAT WERE MADE BY MAN & THE RIGHTEOUSNESS OF GOD IS FAITH, FAITH THAT JESUS IS OUR SAVIOR.

Have you made righteousness a "stumbling block" or a "stepping-stone" in your life?

Reread Philippians 3:10–16, 20-21.

4. Read Romans 6:4-14. In your own words, explain the resurrection power that Paul desired to experience in this life. Are you experiencing this resurrection power in your life? If not, why not?

> BECAUSE CHRIST DIED FOR OUR SINS, WHEN WE ARE BAPTIZED AS CHRISTIANS WE HAVE A SECOND CHANCE TO FOLLOW CHRIST'S TEACHINGS AND NOT BE TEMPTED BY SIN.

5. What resurrection power did Paul look forward to experiencing in eternal life? (Eph. 2:5-9; 1 Cor. 15:42-44, 49) How do both aspects of this resurrection power relate to our joy?

> 1. THAT OF BEING RAISED TO HEAVEN TO BE WITH CHRIST.
> 2. BECAUSE IF WE FOLLOW CHRIST'S TEACHINGS AND LIVE IN ACCORDANCE TO HIS WORD, WE ARE ASSURED OUR PLACE IN HEAVEN.

6. What is the end result of suffering according to Hebrews 5:8-9 and James 1:2-4? In what ways do we benefit when we share in the fellowship of His sufferings? (2 Cor. 1:3-5; 4:8-10; 1 Peter 4:12-14; 5:9-10)

> 1. OBEDIANCE
> 2. OUR COMFORT OVERFLOWS, HARD PRESSED NOT CRUSHED, PERPLEXED NOT IN DESPAIR, PERSECUTED NOT ABANDONED, STRUCK DOWN NOT DESTROYED, & CHRIST WILL MAKE US STRONG, FIRM AND STEADFAST.

7. What goals are you to pursue according to God's high calling for you? (Read 2 Timothy 1:8-9; Ephesians 1:4-5; 2:10; 4:1; Romans 8:28-29; and 1 Thessalonians 4:7.) According to Hebrews 12:2, what "joyful pursuit" was set before Christ?

> 1. NOT BE ASHAMED TO TESTIFY, TO BE HOLY & BLAMELESS, DO GOOD WORKS, TO LIVE A LIFE WORTHY OF THE CALLING WE HAVE REC'D, TO CONFORM TO CHRIST'S LIKENESS & LIVE A HOLY LIFE.
> 2. TO SIT AT THE RIGHT HAND OF THE THRONE OF GOD.

8. What does Acts 20:24 specify was Paul's task to complete? Would you say that Paul joyfully pursued this goal? Evaluate the joy with which you carry out God's purposes for your life.

> 1. TESTIFYING TO THE GOSPEL OF GOD'S GRACE.
> 2. YES
> 3. JUST KNOWING THAT EVERYTHING I DO, EVERY PATH I TAKE IS DIRECTED BY GOD BRINGS ME JOY.

9. In order to persevere in the footrace of life, what must one do, according to verse 13? Why is it necessary to forget the past? (See Hebrews 12:1; Galatians 5:7-8; and 1 Thessalonians 2:18.) Define "forget" in this context.

1. FORGET WHAT IS BEHIND & STRAIN TOWARD WHAT IS AHEAD.
2. BECAUSE WE WON'T BE ABLE TO CONTINUE IN OUR SPIRITUAL GROWTH OTHERWISE.
3. TO NOT GET ENTANGLED WITH OUR OLD SINFUL WAYS.

10. What did Paul need to forget, according to Acts 7:54–8:3? What do you need to forget? How can these Scriptures help you forget the past: 2 Corinthians 5:17; Romans 8:1; 1 Peter 1:22-23; 1 John 1:9; Matthew 6:14-15; and Jeremiah 31:34b?

1. THAT HE IMPRISONED PEOPLE OF THE CHURCH.
2. BITTERNESS
3. AS LONG AS WE ASK FORGIVENESS, CHRIST WILL NOT REMEMBER OUR SINS.

11. What is the prize referred to in Philippians 3:14? Consider the following Scriptures: 1 Corinthians 2:9; 2 Timothy 4:8; 1 Peter 1:4; 5:4; James 1:12; Revelation 22:1-5; and Daniel 12:2-3.

1. ETERNAL LIFE

12. As citizens of heaven, what is our position here on earth as stated in Hebrews 11:13 and 1 Peter 2:11? What is our mission, according to 2 Corinthians 5:20? What does Philippians 3:20 say our attitude is to be while waiting to go home? Is this your attitude? Why or why not?

1. ALIENS, STRANGERS
2. TO BECOME RECONCILED TO GOD.
3. TO EAGERLY AWAIT JESUS' RETURN.

13. Who is the architect and builder of our city? (Heb. 11:10) What is it like? (Rev. 21:10–22:5) What about it gives you the most joy?

1. GOD
2. A HIGH MOUNTAIN CITY WHERE THERE WILL BE NO NIGHTS.
3. BEING IN GOD'S PRESENCE.

🐦 SAVOR GOD'S TRUTH 🐦

In his book *Youth Witness Mission*, Bruce Mitchell tells this story:

A man was lost in the desert. He stumbled along, his throat parched, his lips cracked. Then, there before him was an old water pump. He used his remaining strength to grasp the handle and pump furiously. No water came. In despair, he sat down, too tired and too thirsty to go on. Suddenly, he saw an old, rusty tin can in front of him. In it was a piece of paper, carefully wrapped. He unwrapped the paper and found this note: "This pump has a leather washer. The washer must be wet for the pump to work. Under the big board there is a small bottle of water; just enough to prime the pump. If you drink any of it, there won't be enough to wet the washer. If you pour it all on the washer, you will have water to spare. Signed . . . Desert Pete"[1]

Desert Pete was asking this dying man to give up, in faith, something of extreme value. Desert Pete was promising him a great gain, but the dying man had to first be willing to lose!

In the third chapter of Philippians, we find Paul also in a situation of gaining through losing. In verses 7 and 8, he declares that he has lost all things that were counted as profitable to him in order to gain the priceless privilege of knowing Christ. Paul purposely forfeited everything that might intrude on his total faith in Christ, including his highly regarded Jewish credentials which he states in verses 5 and 7. As a full-blooded Jew, pursuing righteousness by his own efforts and obedience to the Law, Paul counted his Jewish heritage and practices as valuable advantages—until his Damascus Road experience. After his conversion and the discovery of the righteousness of God received by faith, he realized that what he once thought was profitable was really a liability. His Jewish advantages were really disadvantages because they had detrimentally influenced the pursuits of his life. They had caused him not only to pursue a worthless righteousness but also to pursue the persecution of the church.

In Philippians 3:8-16, 20-21, Paul is stating the joyful pursuit that evolved from the reassessment of his spiritual life after he accepted Christ as his Saviour. Paul's pursuit involves gaining the presence of Christ, the perfection of Christ, and the possession of the prize!

When Paul speaks of his desire to gain the knowledge of Christ, he, in essence, means that he wants to continually experience the *presence of Christ* by living in a vital relationship with Him. For Paul, "to know Christ" means to live in intimate, unbroken union and fellowship with Him. Paul's pursuit is to progressively become more deeply acquainted with Christ so as to recognize and experientially understand the wonders of His Person more clearly. In order to gain the surpassing value of this knowledge, Paul surrenders his self-will in order to devote his whole existence to abiding in Christ. Paul loses himself so that he can be found in Christ alone! We learn from Paul that this renunciation of self is necessary if one is to successfully pursue the presence of Christ. In Psalm 16:11, we read, "You have made known to me the path of life; You will fill me with joy in Your presence, with eternal pleasures at Your right hand" (NIV). What about you? Are you experiencing this fullness of joy in your life? If not, begin today to pursue the presence of Christ by following Paul's example.

The second part of Paul's joyful pursuit involves gaining the *perfection of Christ*. God's perfection is absolute, but man's perfection is relative. When Paul talks about being made perfect, he is referring to the completion of his goal of becoming spiritually mature by becoming conformed to Christ (Rom. 8:29). He realizes that the first step in gaining this perfection involves accepting God's free gift of righteousness through faith in His Son (Rom. 10:9-10). In his pursuit, however, Paul does not stop with the righteousness that he has gained through his regeneration. It is his determined purpose to demonstrate his union with Christ by striving to become ever-increasingly conformed to Christ. It is Paul's goal to experience the power of Christ's resurrection and the fellowship of His sufferings in such a way that he will gain a true knowledge of Christlikeness.

Nothing increases one's understanding of something more adequately than "experiential" knowledge. When I was preparing to have my first baby, I read books, talked to people, and Joe and I attended prenatal classes at the hospital. At these classes, we watched films, listened to lectures, read more books, and even practiced delivery techniques. By the time my baby was ready to be born, I had accumulated a lot of intellectual knowledge about childbirth. I felt physically and mentally prepared, and I felt I understood everything very well. My labor pains, however, painted a vivid reminder for me of the difference between intellectual and experiential knowledge! My experience of childbirth definitely increased my understanding of it. It also better prepared me for the birth of my second child.

Paul believes that his experiential knowledge of Christ's suffering and resurrection will better prepare him to successfully pursue the perfection of Christ. First, by sharing in the fellowship of Christ's sufferings, Paul will share in the end result of suffering, which is perfection or maturity in Christ (James 1:4). Suffering will not only bring him to a state of completeness in which he morally lacks nothing, but it will also motivate him to adopt the same perspective of joy that was set forth by Christ in His suffering (Heb. 12:2; James 1:2). Second, by experiencing the resurrection power of Christ, Paul can gain conformity to Christ now and eternally. This conformity takes place now as he depends on the resurrection power of Christ to work in his life, raising him in victory over the death of sin and empowering him to live a new life in Christ. By relying on Christ's power to crucify his old self with its evil practices and to put on his new self, Paul is being renewed in knowledge and understanding according to the image of His Creator (Col. 3:10). Paul realizes, however, that this perfection or complete conformity to Christ will only be obtained at Christ's return. He eagerly awaits the day that he will eternally experience the resurrection power of Christ, as his mortal body is transformed into a glorified body, fashioned in the complete likeness of Christ (1 Cor. 15:49).

How is your experiential knowledge of Christ? Are you as determined as Paul to pursue intimacy with Christ, so that you can become all that God wants you to be?

The third part of Paul's joyful pursuit concerns gaining the *possession of the prize.* Paul makes this last part of his pursuit our pursuit, by his expectation of us, as growing Christians, to adopt his mature attitudes and actions and by his use of first-person-plural pronouns in verses 15-16 and 20-21. Paul never states exactly what the heavenly prize is, but he uses his example, as well as exhortation, to relate to us how to pursue it. By painting a word picture of a footrace, Paul tells us specific actions to take in regard to the past, present, and future in order to take hold of the goals for which God has called us.

First, we, like Paul, must deliberately and continually erase our past experiences—whether failures or triumphs—from our consciousness. We must refuse to allow them to influence our spiritual outlook or impede our progress. We must not let condemnation or pride keep us from obtaining the prize.

Second, each of us must daily live up to the standard of Christian maturity that we have achieved, according to our understanding of

God's truth. This exhortation of Paul's for the present does not, however, lend itself to complacency. We must recognize that it is our continuing responsibility to make spiritual progress our priority. We must neither become careless in our pursuit of spiritual maturity nor conceited, believing that we have completed our growth. We, like Paul, must "press on." We must run the race of life by relentlessly centering all our energy and efforts on the course that God has chosen for us, pushing ourselves toward what is ahead. The eager anticipation of a Saviour, a prize, and a home in heaven enable us, like Paul, to finish our course with joy!

Life offers us the choice of many different pursuits, but not all of them generate joy. God's Word promises that the pursuits of Paul will lead to joy. Assess your goals. Evaluate the measure of your joy. Are you pursuing the presence of Christ? First Peter 1:8 reads, "Though you have not seen Him, you love Him; and even though you do not see Him now, you believe in Him and are filled with an inexpressible and glorious joy, for you are receiving the goal of your faith, the salvation of your souls" (NIV). Are you pursuing the perfection of Christ? In Jude 24, we read, "To Him who is able to keep you from falling and to present you before His glorious presence without fault and with great joy" (NIV). Are you working toward gaining the possession of the prize? In Isaiah 35:9b-10, we find, "But only the redeemed will walk there, and the ransomed of the Lord will return. They will enter Zion with singing; everlasting joy will crown their heads. Gladness and joy will overtake them, and sorrow and sighing will flee away." Fill your life with joyful pursuits!

🍂 *SEASON YOUR LIFE* 🍂

1. Is there anything in your life that is keeping you from gaining Christ? Have you accepted God's gift of righteousness, according to Romans 10:9-10? If not, do so today. If you have, spend time praising Him and thanking Him for His loving-kindness to you.

2. Compare and contrast your pursuits in life before and after you accepted Christ as your Saviour. Have your goals changed? Why or why not? Which of Paul's pursuits need to become a part of your life? How will you make this happen?

3. Is there any deadness in your spiritual life that needs to be resurrected? What will you do this week to pursue a more intimate relationship with Christ and increase your knowledge of Him?

4. Is there sin in your life to which you need to apply the resurrection power of Christ? Spend time in prayer regarding the truth of 1 John 1:9. Meditate on Colossians 3:1-10 and Romans 6. Make it your joyful pursuit to memorize Galatians 2:20 and Romans 13:14 this week.

5. Is there anything in your past that is keeping you from pressing on toward the heavenly prize that awaits you? Is there anything you need to confess? Anything you need to forgive or accept forgiveness for? Are there any feelings of guilt, inadequacy, resentment, or bitterness that need to be healed? Find rest in the everlasting arms of your compassionate Heavenly Father. He deeply cares about you.

6. What have you learned from this lesson that will help you run the race of life with joy?

CHAPTER SEVEN

Peace and Joy

❦ SIMMER THESE THOUGHTS ❦

Read Philippians 4:1-9.

1. Considering what you have learned from Paul, reflect on each section of Scripture that we have studied and write a principle for "standing firm" in the Lord. Try to capture the principle in one sentence.

Philippians 1:1-11 *THRU OUR SPIRITUAL JOURNEY LOVE WILL ABOUND MORE IN KNOWLEDGE TO DISCERN WHAT IS GOOD & WE WILL BECOME PURE & BLAMELESS.*

Philippians 1:12-20 *TRY TO ALWAYS SPEAK THE WORD OF GOD COURAGEOUSLY & FEARLESSLY OUT OF LOVE.*

Philippians 1:21-30 *BE OBEDIENT TO THE GOSPEL OF CHRIST W/O BEING FRIGHTENED IN ANY WAY KNOWING THAT GOD WILL PROTECT & REWARD US FOR OUR FAITH.*

Philippians 2:1-11 *BE LIKE MINDED WITH CHRIST IN HAVING THE SAME LOVE & HUMBLENESS TO CONSIDER OTHERS BETTER THAN OURSELVES & PUT OTHERS FIRST.*

Philippians 2:12–3:3, 17-19 *BE AWARE OF EVIL & DO NOT FALL BACK ON THE WAYS OF MAN BUT ON THE WAYS OF CHRIST.*

Philippians 3:4-16, 20-21 *KEEP ON THE PATH OF YOUR SPIRITUAL JOURNEY & USE THE GIFTS THAT GOD GAVE YOU TO NOT ONLY DO GOOD WORKS BUT TO BRING OTHERS ON OUR SPIRITUAL JOURNEY.*

What advice can be added to this list from Philippians 4:1-9? How is "standing firm" in the Lord related to joy? (Ps. 16:7-11)

REJOICE IN ALL THAT IS GOOD, PURE, NOBLE & ESPECIALLY IN THE LORD & PRAY WITH THANKSGIVING FOR ALL THAT CHRIST HAS DONE FOR US.

59

IF WE STAND FIRM IN THE LORD WE WILL NOT ONLY KNOW GREAT JOY IN THIS LIVE BUT WILL BE ASSURED GREAT JOY FOR ETERNITY.

2. In what ways were the Philippians Paul's "joy and crown"? What is required of us in order for others to become our "joy and crown"? Who is your "joy and crown"?

THE PHILIPPIANS HAD A PARTNERSHIP W/THE
GOSPEL FROM THE FIRST DAY.
TO STAND FIRM IN THE GOSPEL OF CHRIST.

3. Why is Paul concerned about the relationship of Euodia and Syntyche? According to the following Scriptures, what are our responsibilities as believers: 2 Corinthians 13:11; Romans 12:18; 14:19; and 1 Thessalonians 5:13b? Is there anyone with whom you need to pursue peace, but you are unsure about what to do? Follow the advice of James 1:5.

BECAUSE HE LOVES THEM & WANTS THEM TO
BE OF LIKE MINDEDNESS TO CHRIST.
TO AIM FOR PERFECTION, BE OF ONE MIND, LIVE IN PEACE
BE KIND TO EACH OTHER.

4. Check different Bible versions to see how they refer to the person in Philippians 4:3 who is asked to help Euodia and Syntyche. Look up "yokefellow" in a Bible dictionary. What would a yokefellow do to help Euodia and Syntyche? Relate Proverbs 12:20 and Matthew 5:9 to this situation. TEAMMATE

5. Read Matthew 10:32-33; Romans 10:9-10; Revelation 3:5; 20:11-15; 21:27. What is the "Book of Life"? Whose names are written in it? What will happen to them?

IT IS A BOOK WHERE GOD HAS RECORDED ALL OUR
GOOD DEEDS. ONLY THOSE PEOPLE WHO FOLLOWED
CHRIST'S TEACHINGS & OBEYED THESE TEACHINGS.
THEY WILL HAVE ETERNAL LIFE.

6. Whose names are not found in the Book of Life? What will happen to them? Is your name written in the Book of Life?

ANYONE WHO IS IMPURE, WHO DOES WHAT IS
SHAMEFUL OR DECEITFUL.
THEY WILL BE THROWN INTO THE LAKE OF FIRE.

7. What does it mean to "rejoice in the Lord"? (Phil. 4:4) What do you
   think is the key word? What do you learn from the following verses
   concerning this matter of rejoicing: Habakkuk 3:17-19; 1 Thessalonians 5:18; Psalms 34:1; 145:1-2?

   *TO KNOW WHAT CHRIST HAS DONE FOR US IN HIS
   ULTIMATE SACRIFICE ON THE CROSS FOR OUR SINS.
   REJOICE.
   THAT NO MATTER WHAT EACH DAY BRINGS, ALWAYS
   REJOICE & PRAISE THE LORD.*

8. Read Philippians 4:5 in at least two other Bible versions different
   from the one you are using. What does Paul desire to be evident in
   the Philippians' lives? Why? (For another perspective, see 1 Thessalonians 4:16–5:2.) Explain this Christian virtue in relation to Luke
   6:29-35; Titus 3:1-2; and James 5:7-11. *FOREBEARANCE,
   GENTLENESS.
   EMULATE JESUS, BE PREPARED FOR JESUS' COMING
   BE PATIENT W/ONE ANOTHER, PERSEVERE & GO THE
   SECOND MILE.*

9. What does Paul say should be our antidote for worry and anxiety?
   What should accompany this antidote? What will be the end result?
   *PRAYER & PETITION.
   THANKSGIVING
   THE PEACE OF GOD WILL ENVELOPE OUR HEARTS
   & MINDS.*

10. Read Romans 5:1; 15:13; Colossians 1:20; John 14:27; 16:33;
    Philippians 4:7; Ephesians 2:14-17; and Isaiah 9:6-7. Then explain
    the following phrases and how they relate to each other: "peace
    with God"; "peace of God"; and the "God of peace."

11. In Philippians 4:8-9, what two things does Paul exhort the Philippi-
    ans, as well as us, to do? What will be the end result? Read Genesis
    6:5-6; Proverbs 15:26; 23:7a; Matthew 15:17-18; and Romans 8:6.
    How does our thought life affect our relationship with God, our
    peace, and our joy? *TO THINK ABOUT WHATEVER IS TRUE
    NOBLE, RIGHT, PURE, LOVELY, ADMIRABLE, EXCELLENT &
    PRAISE WORTHY & TO PUT INTO PRACTICE EVERYTHING WE'VE
    LEARNED, HEARD, REC'D OR SEEN IN PAUL. THE GOD
    OF PEACE WILL BE WITH US.
    THE HUMAN THOUGHT*

❧ SAVOR GOD'S TRUTH ❧

The crowd cheers ecstatically! His crew members and family press around him! Radio announcers and reporters push toward him as he is lifted out of his car! He begins to drink the traditional bottle of milk while a wreath of laurel, a mark of victory and honor, is placed around his neck. Such is the scenario every May in Victory Lane at the Indianapolis 500! It is here that the winner of this well-known racing event is crowned. He proudly wears his festive garland as a sign of gladness and celebration!

In chapter 4 of Philippians, we see Paul expressing similar gladness and reason for celebration concerning the Philippians, as he refers to them as his "joy and crown." The Greek word for "crown" was commonly used to create a word picture of the laurel wreath awarded to the winner of an athletic contest. The Philippians are Paul's present joy as they continue to grow spiritually and live in faithful service. They will be his future crown when Christ rewards His servants at the final day. Their souls in heaven will be living evidence of Paul's apostleship and proof of the value of his labors.

Paul teaches that this triumph of grace, however, must be accompanied by the steadfastness of the saints. He has throughout his letter to the Philippians given them principles to follow in order to stand firm in the Lord. In Philippians 4:1-9, Paul continues his advice to the Philippians by instructing them in regard to peaceful living. Paul realizes that standing firm will allow the Philippians to maintain the joy of their salvation. In this first part of chapter 4, we see that it is Paul's desire for the Philippians to experience the joy of living in *peace with others* and in *peace within themselves,* while experiencing *peace with God as well.*

In verses 2, 3, and 5, Paul makes a plea for the Philippians to live in *peace with others*—fellow believers as well as unbelievers. He first addresses a problem of disunity which has developed between two women of the church fellowship whom he esteems as his coworkers for the cause of the Gospel. He admonishes Euodia and Syntyche to have the like-mindedness that he had instructed them about in Philippians 2:3-5. He pleads with them to live in harmony, sharing an attitude of mutual love, while putting the purposes of the church above personal interests.

Paul's concern for Euodia and Syntyche's reconciliation is so great that he enlists the help of a third party, a yokefellow, to ensure peace between them. "Yokefellow" was a common word used by Greek writers to refer to those who were united by close bonds. Paul wants another Philippian Christian who is familiar with the situation to serve as a peacemaker for these two women. He has previously instructed the Philippians concerning the necessity for unity among fellow laborers of the Gospel who, because they have been saved by grace, have their names recorded in the register of heaven, the Book of Life.

Second, Paul exhorts the Philippians to extend their attitude of peace to unbelievers by commanding them to show "gentleness . . . to all" (NIV). This gentleness must include fair-mindedness as well as forbearance. It is the display of a gracious spirit, resulting from the grace of God, which reflects genuine joy in the Lord. Paul realizes that this virtue may seem impossible to maintain while under the attack of merciless adversaries. Thus, Paul encourages the Philippians by focusing their attention on the Lord's return which holds glorious prospects for them as believers.

To what extent are you experiencing peace with others? Is there anyone with whom you need to be reconciled? How do you respond to disputes among your Christian friends? Are you willing to let God use you as a yokefellow? Proverbs 12:20 tells us that there is joy for those who promote peace.

In Philippians 4:4, 6-7, Paul tells the Philippians how to experience *peace within themselves*. He first gives them a double command to rejoice. Regardless of their circumstances, Paul expects the Philippians to follow his example and maintain a spirit of joy in the Lord. Paul's appeal for joy is in reality a call for faith. Faith in the Lord is necessary in order for joy to triumph over despair. Paul wants the Philippians to consider God's will as their ultimate joy and to trust God to work things out for their good and His glory. Their faith and joy will allow them to experience inner peace in all situations.

Second, Paul commands the Philippians to not fret or worry about anything. Anxiety can poison hearts and minds. The antidote that Paul gives for anxiety is *prayer*. Prayer ensures the well-being of hearts and minds by making available the peace of God which will watch over and protect them like a soldier standing guard at a garrison. Paul instructs the Philippians to pray about everything, approaching God in an attitude of worship, expressing their needs, and making definite requests. He emphasizes that these prayers and petitions must be made with an attitude of thankfulness that springs forth from a deliberate recalling of God's faithfulness and mercy. If the Philippians follow Paul's instructions, he promises them that God will place His own unique peace within them that is so great that it goes beyond human comprehension!

Last summer, I was sitting in a screened-in porch, which is separated from our house, when a sudden storm hit! The strong winds howled as they bent the trees and sent the rain crashing against the screens. The lightning, which cracked loudly in the dark sky, was accompanied by great rumbles of thunder. The birds that had been eating peacefully at my feeders noisily screeched warnings as they sought refuge. The openness of the porch gave me little protection as I sat uneasily in the midst of the storm. As quickly as it came, the storm seemed to end.

As I made my way to the house, I suddenly stopped when I became astonishingly aware of the overwhelming tranquility that followed the storm. The calmness and serenity that surrounded me was in awesome contrast to the ferociousness of the storm displayed moments before! Those moments of peace became etched within my mind. These verses in Philippians tell us that God is able to etch a peace within our hearts even greater than that following the storm!

Do you need to experience the peace of God within your life today? This peace of God is available to all who have found peace with God by being justified by faith in Christ (Rom. 8:1). If you have experienced God's saving grace and yet struggle with worry and anxiety, begin today to follow Paul's advice: Rejoice and pray! We are told in Isaiah 26:3 that God will keep in perfect peace those whose minds are steadfast because they trust in Him.

In Philippians 4:8-9, Paul tells the Philippians how to continue to live in *peace with God* who, as the God of peace, reconciled them to Himself through the Cross (Eph. 2:16). He commands them to let their thoughts and actions reflect not only the God of peace, but also the peace of God—both of which abide within them. He wants the peace of God to rule their hearts (Col. 3:15), just like an umpire deciding which thoughts and actions are "safe" and which are "out" according to the rule book of life, the Bible! Paul realizes that the Philippians will enjoy God's peace only to the extent that they live in obedience to Him, and that their inner tranquility indicates the degree to which they are living in peace with Him. Paul does not want God to say of the Philippians what He said of the Israelites in Isaiah 1:2b: "I reared children and brought them up, but they have rebelled against Me" (NIV). Paul's desire is for the Philippians to continuously live in harmony with God by developing a righteous thought life. He instructs them to fix their minds on excellent and praiseworthy things, knowing that their thoughts will shape their behavior into righteous actions and that their righteousness will let them live in peace. Isaiah 32:17 (AMP) reads, "And the effect of righteousness shall be peace [internal and external], and the result of righteousness, quietness and confident trust for ever."

Are you living in peace with God or are you behaving like a rebellious child? Do your thoughts and actions reveal a love for righteousness? Following Paul's advice will lead you to both peace and joy. In Hebrews 1:9, we read, "You have loved righteousness and hated wickedness; therefore, God, your God, has set you above your companions by anointing you with the oil of joy" (NIV).

Paul's counsel to the Philippians teaches us that real peace and joy come only from Christ dwelling within us. Whether we need peace with others, peace within, or peace with God, we must pursue it through Christ, who is our peace—our bond of unity and harmony. "May the God of your hope so fill you with all joy and peace in believing—through the experience of your faith—that by the power of the Holy Spirit you may abound and be overflowing (bubbling over) with hope" (Rom. 15:13, AMP).

❧ SEASON YOUR LIFE ❧

1. Are you standing firm in the Lord? Evaluate your performance according to the principles that you wrote in question 1 of "Simmer These Thoughts." What will you do this week to gain firmer footing in your Christian walk?

2. Evaluate your attitude of rejoicing. Do you find yourself rejoicing in the Lord, or in other things? Do you allow circumstances in your life to keep you from rejoicing? What steps do you need to take in order to rejoice in the Lord always? For the next seven days, read and meditate on one of the following Scriptures each day: Psalms 103; 145; 146; 147; 148; 149; 150.

3. Look for opportunities this week to manifest a gentle, forbearing spirit toward those who seem to make life difficult for you.

4. Make a list of the things in your life that cause you anxiety. Take this list before the Lord in prayer. First, spend time expressing your love to God and offering praise. Then, use your list to make definite requests as you express your needs. Be sure to thank God for His goodness and faithfulness. Express trust and faith, and thank Him for working His perfect will in your life.

5. What types of thoughts occupy your mind? Meditate on 2 Corinthians 10:5. Ask the Lord to reveal to you things in your life that contribute negatively to your thoughts. Ask God's help this week in being alert to your thought life. Practice capturing your negative and/or evil thoughts and making them obedient to Christ by following Paul's pattern for thinking in Philippians 4:8.

CHAPTER EIGHT

Power and Joy

🔥 SIMMER THESE THOUGHTS 🔥

Read Philippians 4:10-23. Reread 4:12-13.

1. What secret ingredient for life did Paul discover that leads to contentment? (Read 2 Corinthians 1:8-10; 6:1-10; 11:23-28.) Describe the circumstances in which Paul had to learn contentment and the ways in which he responded to these circumstances.

CHRIST, JESUS.
ENDURANCE, HARDSHIPS, BEATINGS, INPRISONMENT, RIOTS
HARD WORK, SLEEPLESS NIGHTS, HUNGER, UNDERSTANDING,
PATIENCE, KINDNESS, STONED, SHIPWRECKED,
HE RELIED ON JESUS FOR STRENGTH & TO DELIVER HIM FROM HIS
PERILS.

2. Why was Paul able to respond with contentment? Meditate on 1 Timothy 6:6. What would you say are some of the "great gains" of godliness with contentment?

BECAUSE HE CAME TO RELY ON GOD FOR EVERYTHING, SO
IT DIDN'T MATTER IF HE WAS RICH OR POOR, HUNGRY OR
WELL FED.
IF WE LIVE AS CHRIST TEACHES US, WE SHALL WANT
FOR NOTHING & WE WILL HAVE EVERLASTING LIFE WITH HIM.

Read Ephesians 3:16-17; 2 Corinthians 12:9-10; Nehemiah 8:10b; Isaiah 40:28-31.

3. Explain in your own words how the Lord strengthens us. Share how Philippians 4:13 has been a reality in your life.

IF WE RELY ON THE LORD INSTEAD OF OURSELVES
ESPECIALLY WHERE WE ARE THE WEAKEST, THE LORD
WILL STRENGTHEN US.

Reread Philippians 4:10-23.

4. Why was Paul rejoicing in verse 10? In whom? (James 1:17) Why had it been a while since the Philippians had expressed their

BECAUSE THE PHILIPPIANS SHOWED CONCERN FOR
PAUL WHEN HE WAS IN NEED, IN THE LORD.

67

concern for Paul? How had they helped Paul in the past? How and to what extent were they meeting his needs now?

BECAUSE THEY HAD NO WAY TO SHOW THEIR
CONCERN. THEY AMPLY SUPPLIED PAUL WITH
AID WHEN HE WAS IN NEED.

5. According to Philippians 4:17, what did Paul feel was the greatest benefit of the Philippians' gift? How did they profit because of their giving? (Prov. 11:25; 19:17; Matt. 5:7; 25:34-40; Luke 6:38; Heb. 6:10) How can you apply these truths to your own life?

HE WANTED TO CREDIT THEIR ACCOUNT SO
THEY WOULD PROSPER & BE REWARDED THEIR INHERITANCE
IN THE KINGDOM OF GOD.

6. According to 2 Corinthians 9:6-8, what is the relationship between "joy" and "giving"? What are the results? Are you a cheerful giver?

BECAUSE GOD LOVES A CHEERFUL GIVER & ~~IT IS~~ GIVING,
IS PLEASING TO HIM, SO TOO WILL GOD GIVE
TO THOSE WHO GIVE.

7. How does Paul describe the Philippians' gift in 4:18? Why is this significant? (Gen. 8:20-21; Lev. 1:8-9; 7:12-15; Eph. 5:2; Rom. 12:1; Heb. 13:15-16; 1 Peter 2:5)

AS A FRAGRANT OFFERING.
BECAUSE GIVING WITHOUT WANTING OR EXPECTING,
ANYTHING IN RETURN IS PLEASING TO GOD

8. What special promise does Paul give the Philippians in 4:19? How can this promise be an encouragement to you? What do you think is the most important word in this promise? Why?

THAT GOD WILL MEET ALL THEIR NEEDS, ACCORDING
TO HIS GLORIOUS RICHES IN CHRIST JESUS.

9. How would you describe "His glorious riches" (NIV) or "His riches in glory"? (KJV) (See Ephesians 1:7, 18; 3:8, 16-21; Romans 11:33; and 2 Corinthians 8:9.)

JESUS DIED FOR OUR SINS SO THAT WE
MAY BE STRENGTHENED BY HIM & HAVE
EVERLASTING LIFE WITH HIM.

10. How is Philippians 4:21-22 reflective of the unity that God has established between believers everywhere? (See 2 Corinthians 6:16-18; Galatians 3:26; Romans 8:15b-16.) How will the reality of Paul's final prayer in Philippians 4:23 sustain unity among the Philippian congregation?

11. How will the reality of 4:23 in the lives of the Philippians influence their joy? Relate that verse to Colossians 1:9-14.

12. Briefly review the eight lessons in this Bible study. Write concise instructions (one or two sentences) from each lesson that tell "how to spice up your life with joy":

Lesson 1: Joyful Prayer

Lesson 2: Joyful Praise

Lesson 3: Joyful Purpose

Lesson 4: Partnership in Joy

Lesson 5: Pattern for Joy

Lesson 6: Joyful Pursuit

Lesson 7: Peace and Joy

Lesson 8: Power and Joy

Are there any instructions that you have written that you are not putting into practice?

🐚 SAVOR GOD'S TRUTH 🐚

It was the best cheesecake that I had ever tasted! What made it so unusually delicious? A few bites revealed that there were nuts in the crust. They definitely appealed to my taste buds, and yet, I knew that the full flavor difference was due to something else. I could not decide what it was. I asked my friend Karen to reveal the "secret" ingredients that made her cheesecake unique. The "secret" ingredients turned out to be cinnamon and almond extract, neither of which I had ever used when making a cheesecake. Needless to say, I have used her recipe instead of mine ever since!

In the fourth chapter of Philippians, Paul announces that he has discovered life's secret ingredient. In verse 13, he states, "I can do everything through Him who gives me strength" (NIV). I especially love the way this verse is stated in *The Amplified New Testament:* "I have strength for all things in Christ who empowers me—I am ready for anything and equal to anything through Him who infuses inner strength into me [that is, I am self-sufficient in Christ's sufficiency]." The indwelling Christ is the treasured ingredient in Paul's life. Through the inner strengthening of Christ, Paul experiences a power that satisfies, supplies, and sustains. He tells about this power and his joy in Philippians 4:10-23.

Paul speaks of the *power that satisfies* in verses 11-13. His close fellowship with Christ, who abides within him, activates the power that Paul needs in order to be content in all circumstances. Second Corinthians 4:7 reads, "But we have this treasure in earthen vessels, that the surpassing greatness of the power may be of God and not from ourselves." It is Christ who teaches Paul how to live victoriously in whatever situations are in God's will for him. The person of Jesus Christ enables Paul to maintain priorities and a perspective that ensure contentment. Paul's focus is continually on things above. He is able to concentrate on the eternal and the invisible instead of the temporal and the visible (2 Cor. 4:18). He lives for the cause of Christ and not for the cause of self by giving up all rights to his life here on earth. The power of Christ enables Paul to experience and maintain a consistent level of true satisfaction. Paul could be classified as a "thermostat" believer instead of a "thermometer" believer! *Wilmington's Guide to the Bible* explains the difference:

1. The "thermometer" believer. His satisfaction is totally dependent upon outside circumstances. He simply registers the prevailing spiritual temperature.
2. The "thermostat" believer. His satisfaction is totally independent of the outside circumstances. He is not only unaffected by it, but actually controls that area surrounding him.[1]

What about you? Are you a "thermometer" believer or a "thermostat" believer? Try applying this idea to the matter of joy as well as satisfaction. Do you register your joy on a thermometer or do you control it with a thermostat? I believe that one of the "great gains" of godliness with contentment (1 Tim. 6:6) is "thermostatic" joy!

In Philippians 4:10, 14-20, Paul tells how his needs have been met by the *power that supplies*. The Philippians had sent Paul generous financial help by means of Epaphroditus that had amply met his needs. It was common for the Philippians to express their partnership with Paul by means of their gifts, but they had not had an opportunity to do so for quite some time. Paul is thankful for their support, and yet, their concern for him and their obedience to God, fragrantly expressed in their giving, causes him more joy than the gift itself. Paul, however, gives glory where glory is due. He rejoices not in the Philippians but in the Lord who has met his needs *through* the Philippians. Paul realizes that it is the power of the Holy Spirit that prompts believers to meet the needs of other believers. God welcomes and delights in the sacrificial offerings given as acts of worship from obedient hearts.

To all who joyously display spiritual maturity by generously investing in the kingdom of God, rich dividends are promised (2 Cor. 9:6-8). This promise is stated by Paul in verse 19, "And my God will meet all your needs according to His glorious riches in Christ Jesus" (NIV). Our union with Christ makes available to us the full wealth of God which is revealed in His mercy and redemption. Through His provisional power, God not only meets our material needs but also our spiritual, mental, and physical needs.

We must remember, however, that God responds to our needs according to His wisdom and His timetable. When His disciples asked Jesus questions regarding how and when He would meet the needs of Israel, Jesus gave them this answer in Acts 1:7 (AMP): "He said to them,

'It is not for you to become acquainted with and know what time brings—the things and events of time and their definite periods—fixed years and seasons (their critical nick of time), which the Father has appointed (fixed and reserved) by His own choice and authority and personal power.' "

We, like Paul, must have faith that God's power will supply our needs, but we must trust Him with the details of our provisional care! Hebrews 11:1 reads, "Faith is being sure of what we hope for and certain of what we do not see" (NIV). Our trust will cause us to express praise and thanksgiving to God for His goodness and faithfulness, just as Paul does in verse 20.

What is the most pressing need in your life today? Embrace the truth of Philippians 4:19 with faith! Replace anxiety and impatience with praise and thanksgiving, as you wait expectantly to experience the results of God's power as it supplies.

Paul's final greetings to the Philippians, in 4:21-23, are reflective of a *power that sustains*. All of those in whom God's spirit resides are children of God and part of the family of God. Thus, all believers everywhere become brothers and sisters in Christ. The power that links believers together in these bonds of Christ also preserves unity in these relationships, regardless of geographical, cultural, economic, or social factors. Paul's final prayer for his beloved Philippians is that the grace of Christ will be with their spirits. Paul realizes that if the grace of God continues to rule within the inner beings of the Philippians, the results would have sustaining effects. As the spirit of each Philippian believer remains sensitive to God's grace, harmony will be maintained within the Philippian congregation, and peace will dwell within the Philippians as individuals. The power of the indwelling Christ, made available by God's grace, would enable the Philippians to imitate Christ and motivate them to serve others—both of which would generate joy. Paul knew Christ as the sustaining power of his life and the source of his joy. He prayed no less for his Philippian friends whom he cherished.

Do you know Christ as the sustaining power in your life? Is He the source of joy? As your sister in Christ, I would like to pray this prayer for you which is found in Ephesians 3:14-21 (AMP):

> For this reason [seeing the greatness of this plan by which you are built together in Christ], I bow my knees before the Father of our Lord Jesus Christ, for whom every family in heaven and on earth is named—[that Father] from whom all fatherhood takes its title and derives its name. May He grant you out of the rich treasury of His glory to be strengthened

and reinforced with mighty power in the inner man by the (Holy) Spirit [Himself]—indwelling your innermost being and personality. May Christ through your faith [actually] dwell—settle down, abide, make His permanent home—in your hearts! May you be rooted deep in love and founded securely on love, that you may have the power and be strong to apprehend and grasp with all the saints (God's devoted people, the experience of that love) what is the breadth and length and height and depth [of it]; [that you may really come] to know—practically, through experience for yourselves—the love of Christ, which far surpasses mere knowledge (without experience); that you may be filled (through all your being) unto all the fullness of God—[that is] may have the richest measure of the divine Presence, and become a body wholly filled and flooded with God Himself! Now to Him who, by (in consequence of) the [action of His] power that is at work within us, is able to [carry out His purpose and] do superabundantly, far over and above all that we [dare] ask or think—infinitely beyond our highest prayers, desires, thoughts, hopes or dreams—to Him be glory in the church and in Christ Jesus throughout all generations, for ever and ever. Amen—so be it."

As this prayer becomes a reality in your life, you will realize that you, like Paul, have discovered life's secret ingredient which will, in turn, "spice up your life with joy"!

❧ *SEASON YOUR LIFE* ❧

1. Are you content? If your answer is yes, spend time praising God that you, like Paul, are enjoying the benefits of life's secret ingredient. If your answer is no, make a list of what you think would make you content. Then ask yourself these questions:

☐ Am I seeking contentment through eternal or earthly treasures?

☐ Am I more interested in what I can do for God or in what God can do for me?

☐ What am I living for? (God, self, husband, children, etc.)

☐ What have I tried to fill my emptiness with in the past? Has it worked? Why or why not?

Prayerfully consider what changes you need to make in your life that will lead you to the joyful state of contentment.

2. Is there a situation in your life today in which you feel inadequate? How will you apply the truth of Philippians 4:13 in order to overcome your circumstances?

3. Do you consider your giving to be an act of worship? Is the goal of your stewardship to please God? Are you overlooking opportunities to support those who are working for the cause of Christ? Prayerfully evaluate the "fragrance" of your giving.

4. What is your most pressing need today? Memorize Philippians 4:19. Spend time praising God for His provisional care for you!

5. Have you experienced increased joy in your life because of this study? Why or why not? Consider the instructions for joy that you wrote in question 8 of "Simmer These Thoughts." Evaluate your joy using your own instructions. What goals can you set for yourself in the area of joy? Write them down. Periodically check your progress even though you have finished this Bible study!

Chapter 6
1. Bruce Mitchell, *Youth Witness Mission* (Nashville, Tenn.: Tidings, 1972), pp. 31–32.

Chapter 8
1. Dr. H.L. Wilmington, *Wilmington's Guide to the Bible* (Wheaton, Ill.: Tyndale House Publishers, Inc., 1982), p. 487.

❧ THE LEADER'S RECIPE ❧

The following leader's guide provides you with specific suggestions to facilitate group discussion. You will find it most helpful if you encourage people to do the study before the group meeting. The objectives of this study are: first, to acquaint people with what the Bible actually says; and second, to show how the Bible applies to the practical problems of modern life. Go over the questions in class. Encourage discussion, but try to keep the discussion centered on the lesson, avoiding tangents. Remind group members that the more time they spend studying the lesson, the more interesting and informed the discussion will be.

As each session comes to a close, help group members discuss and draw conclusions that are practical and applicable to their individual lives. Also spend time sharing and praying for each other. This will increase the benefit each group member gains from this study.

General Guidelines for Facilitating
Good Group Discussion

☐ Encourage discussion by asking several group members to contribute answers to a question. "What do the rest of you think?" or "Is there anything else which could be added?" are two ways of doing this.

☐ Be open and warm toward all contributions. Never bluntly reject what anyone says, even if you think the answer is incorrect. Instead, ask what the others in the group think.

☐ As group leader, be sure not to talk too much yourself. Try to redirect questions which you are asked. A discussion should move back and forth between members. The leader is to act as a moderator. As members of a group get to know one another better, the discussion will move more freely.

☐ Don't be afraid of pauses or long silences. People need time to think about the questions. Never answer your own question—either rephrase it or move on to another area for discussion.

☐ Watch hesitant members for an indication by facial expression or bodily posture that they have something to say; then give them an encouraging nod or speak their names.

☐ Discourage too-talkative members from monopolizing the discussion by specifically directing questions to others. If necessary, speak privately to the over-talkative one about the need for discussion, and enlist her help in encouraging all to participate.

General Guidelines for Group Leaders

Preparation

☐ Pray for the Holy Spirit's guidance as you study, that you will be equipped to teach the lesson and make it appealing and applicable.

☐ Read through the entire lesson and any Bible passages or verse that are mentioned. Answer all the questions.

☐ Become familiar enough with the lesson that, if time in the group is running out, you know which question could most easily be left out.

☐ Gather all the items you will need for the study: name tags, extra pens, extra Bibles.

The Meeting

☐ Start and end on time.

☐ Have everyone wear a name tag until group members know one another's names.

☐ Have each group member introduce herself or ask regular attenders to introduce guests.

☐ For each meeting, plan an activity (or ask an icebreaker question) to help group members get to know one another better.

🐚 THE LEADER'S RECIPE 1 🐚

Objective
To help group members evaluate joy and discover its relationship to intercessory prayer.

Personal Preparation
☐ Complete the "Simmer These Thoughts" section for Chapter 1.
☐ Read "Savor God's Truth" for Chapter 1.
☐ Evaluate your own prayer life. Is it "self-centered" or "other-centered"? How could you improve your prayer life?
☐ Spend time praying for each group member.
☐ Prayerfully evaluate your joyfulness. Do you need more joy in your life? Is your joy consistent? How would others evaluate your joyfulness? What could you do to make your joy more complete?
☐ Make sure that you have name tags for your group members. The tags will be used in a specific way at the end of the lesson. Also have available a small basket or container.

Group Participation
☐ Review Paul's circumstances at the time he was writing to the Philippians. Then ask, "What feelings might Paul have experienced as a prisoner in chains?" Discuss what attitudes Paul shows in Philippians 1:1-11. Emphasize Paul's concern in a difficult situation for others rather than himself.
☐ Encourage group members to share about individuals they know personally who manifest joy and unselfish attitudes and actions, regardless of their circumstances.
☐ Have group members share answers to question 6 from the "Simmer These Thoughts" section.
☐ Have someone read aloud Romans 5:1-9. Discuss joy in relation to this passage.
☐ Ask: What can we learn from Paul in Philippians 1:3-11 concerning how to effectively pray for each other?
☐ Have group members share their answers to question 8 from "Simmer These Thoughts." Ask, "How does intercessory prayer fit into our discussion?"
☐ Direct group members to scan Philippians 1:1-11 and choose a verse that best summarizes the session. They should also explain their choices.
☐ Have the group members think of different people who are

sources of joy to them. Before you close with prayer, have members bow their heads, and give those who desire a chance to thank God for one of their sources of joy.

☐ Before group members leave, have them remove their name tags and put them into the basket or container that you brought. Have each individual draw out a name tag. The person whose name a member draws out will be her prayer target for the week. Members should intercede for each other daily in this way.

🕭 *THE LEADER'S RECIPE 2* 🕭

Objective
To encourage group members to praise the Lord in *all* circumstances by focusing their attention on the joy of sharing the Gospel.

Personal Preparation
☐ Complete "Simmer These Thoughts" for Chapter 2.
☐ Read "Savor God's Truth" for Chapter 2.
☐ Use the "Season Your Life" section of Chapter 2 as your spiritual preparation for leading this lesson. Make sure to set aside adequate time to complete all parts of this section before the group meets.
☐ Spend time in prayer, asking God to make you sensitive to the spiritual and emotional needs of the individuals in your group. Ask for wisdom and discernment as to your role in meeting these needs.
☐ If possible, go to a Christian bookstore and buy Campus Crusade's tract *The Four Spiritual Laws*, or Billy Graham's tract *Steps to Peace with God*. Familiarize yourself with either of these presentations of the Gospel. If possible, buy enough copies of either tract to be able to give one to each member of the group.

Group Participation
☐ Invite group members to share answers to question 2 from the "Simmer These Thoughts" section. Ask, "Can any of you share a time when a circumstance in your life was used to promote the Gospel? How did you feel?"
☐ Have group members share their answers to question 4 from "Simmer These Thoughts." Discuss the importance of each of us being able to present the Gospel message accurately. Depending on your preparation, do *one* of the following at this time.
A. Make *The Four Spiritual Laws* or *Steps to Peace with God* familiar to members as a tool for accurately presenting the Gospel. Read through or summarize the tract you bring. When you come to the salvation prayer, have members bow their heads, and say, "If any-one here has never asked Jesus into his or her life as personal Saviour, you may do so now by praying this prayer silently in your heart as I pray it aloud." Then lead in the prayer found in the tract you are using. If you distributed tracts, tell members to keep them and pray for an opportunity to use them in witnessing this week.
B. Or, call the group's attention to part B of "Season Your Life." Present the Gospel to the group using the Scriptures found there.

Ask, "Have you accepted Jesus as your personal Saviour? If not, you may do so today by praying this prayer with your heart as I pray it aloud." Pray the prayer in part B.

☐ Have group members share their answers to questions 6, 8, 9, and 10 from "Simmer These Thoughts." Complete one question before moving to the next.

☐ Tell group members to scan Philippians 1:12-20. They should each choose a verse that best summarizes the session, then explain their choices.

☐ As you close, lead members in a time of *silent* prayer by saying, "Bow your heads, close your eyes, and focus on a difficult circumstance in your life. Discuss your attitudes concerning this circumstance silently with the Lord. Ask Him to show you this week how you can begin to use this circumstance as an opportunity to share Him with others." Second, say that anyone who wishes may offer praise aloud to the Lord (rather than asking petitions from Him). Finally, you pray for the group.

🍂 THE LEADER'S RECIPE 3 🍂

Objective
To motivate group members to make Christ their reason for living.

Personal Preparation
- ☐ Complete "Simmer These Thoughts" for Chapter 3.
- ☐ Read "Savor God's Truth" for Chapter 3.
- ☐ Meditate on Philippians 1:25. Are you willing to commit yourself as deeply to your group members as Paul committed himself to the Philippians? Do you see evidences that your group members are progressing in their faith and joy because of your leadership? Spend time in prayer for each one of your group members.
- ☐ Use Parts 1, 3, and 5 of the "Season Your Life" section of Chapter 3 as your spiritual preparation for teaching this lesson.

Group Participation
- ☐ Have group members share their answers for question 2 from "Simmer These Thoughts."
- ☐ Have group members share their answers for question 3 from the "Simmer These Thoughts" section.
- ☐ Have group members share their answers for question 4 from "Simmer These Thoughts." Discuss the differences involved in living by desires and living by decisions. Ask, "Would anyone be willing to share a time when the Lord enabled you to victoriously live according to a decision you had made rather than giving in to your inner desires?"
- ☐ Have group members discuss their answers to question 5 from "Simmer These Thoughts."
- ☐ Ask, "How does question 7 relate to having a purpose in your life? How will this purpose affect your joy?"
- ☐ Have the group members share their answers to question 8 from "Simmer These Thoughts."
- ☐ Direct group members to scan Philippians 1:21-30 and choose a verse that best summarizes the session.
- ☐ Discuss ways that you, as a group, could contend together for the Gospel of Christ. If possible, choose a specific outreach or evangelism idea and carry it out during the remainder of weeks that you meet as a group.
- ☐ Ask, "How can suffering be part of our joyful purpose for life? How does making Christ our reason for living help us in our suffering?"
- ☐ Close with prayer.

♘ THE LEADER'S RECIPE 4 ♘

Objective
To inspire group members to strive for unity within the body of Christ by imitating the humility of Christ.

Personal Preparation
   ☐ Complete the "Simmer These Thoughts" section for Chapter 4.
   ☐ Read "Savor God's Truth" for Chapter 4.
   ☐ Complete Parts 1, 2, 4, and 6 from "Season Your life" as part of your spiritual preparation for teaching this lesson.
   ☐ Prayerfully consider the extent to which you are involved in the interests and needs of the individual group members as well as the group as a whole. Evaluate yourself as a model of humility for group members. Ask yourself if they would do well to follow your example. Pray that the Lord would make you a teacher with a servant spirit.
   ☐ Prayerfully evaluate the degree of unity and harmony within your group. In what ways can you encourage attitudes and actions of humility among the group members?
   ☐ Pray that the spiritual truths of this lesson will produce life-changing results and lasting fruit in the lives of the individual group members.

Group Participation
   ☐ Have group members share their answers to question 1 from "Simmer These Thoughts."
   ☐ Have group members share their answers to question 2 from the "Simmer These Thoughts" section.
   ☐ Ask, "Will someone share with us how you have recently experienced the joy of our partnership in Christ through the actions or attitudes of a fellow Christian?"
   ☐ Discuss answers to questions 3, 5, 6, 7, and 8 from "Simmer These Thoughts." Complete one question before moving on to the next.
   ☐ Tell group members to choose a verse from Philippians 2:1-11 that best summarizes the session, then to explain their choices to the others.
   ☐ Have group members form a circle and hold hands. Lead the group in singing a song emphasizing Christian unity, such as "Blest Be the Tie That Binds." Ask for personal prayer requests at this time. Close with prayer, making sure to include the spoken requests in your prayer.
   ☐ Before members leave the circle, say, "I would like for us to take

time to 'pamper our partnership' in the Lord. I will show you what to do. Just follow my example." You then turn to the person on your left. Hold the person's hands, look her in the eyes, and say, "I love you, and God loves you. We share a partnership in joy!" Then give the person a hug. She then turns to the person on her left and does the same thing. The words and actions are passed around the circle, with everyone participating in turn. The activity ends after the person on your right hugs you.

In case your group at this session happens to be mixed, use discretion with this activity. You might consider modifying the words or gestures so that, while they would still convey the closeness we have in Christ, you would also avoid uncomfortable feelings among those who take part.

✿ THE LEADER'S RECIPE 5 ✿

Objective
To motivate group members to imitate examples of godliness.

Personal Preparation
☐ Complete the "Simmer These Thoughts" section for Chapter 5. Optional: Using a Bible commentary and a study Bible, do additional study concerning the drink offerings referred to in Philippians 2:17, and the term "dogs" used in Philippians 3:2.
☐ Read "Savor God's Truth" for Chapter 5.
☐ Complete Parts 1, 2, and 4 of the "Season Your Life" section as part of your spiritual preparation for teaching this lesson on imitating examples of godliness.
☐ As a group leader, in what ways do you need to become more like Timothy? Can you classify yourself as a "preferred and proven" group leader? Why or why not? How could imitating Epaphroditus' example make you a better leader? Decide specific things you will do this week to imitate the attitudes and/or actions of Paul, Timothy, and Epaphroditus toward your group members.
☐ Read Hebrews 3:12-13; 10:23-25; Galatians 6:1-6. Prayerfully consider how you can continue to help your group members in the ongoing task of "working out" their salvation. Besides this study, what other opportunities for spiritual growth can you make available to them?
☐ If possible, bring a small, battery-operated toy car for an object lesson.

Group Participation
☐ Have group members share their answers to question 1 from "Simmer These Thoughts." Ask, "Who in your life has provided you with a pattern of Christian living? How did this example cause you to draw closer to God?" Allow individuals in the group to share from their experience.
☐ Have group members share their answers to question 3 from "Simmer These Thoughts." Ask, "What is the correlation between the work we do and the work God does in relation to our salvation? Read the illustration of the battery-powered toy car from the "Savor God's Truth" section, or demonstrate it if you were able to bring a toy car along.
☐ Have group members share their answers to questions 5–10 from "Simmer These Thoughts." Complete one question before moving on to the next.

☐ Instruct group members to choose one verse from Philippians 2:12–3:3, 17-19 that summarizes the session.

☐ Close by reading aloud the questions from Part 2 from the "Season Your Life" section. Do *not* discuss the questions, but use them as challenging thoughts for the group members to consider in the days to come.

☐ Close with prayer.

❧ *THE LEADER'S RECIPE 6* ❧

Objective
To motivate group members to pursue the full, experiential knowledge of Christ.

Personal Preparation
 ☐ Complete the "Simmer These Thoughts" section for Chapter 6. Optional: Using a Bible commentary, do additional study to gain a better understanding of Paul's credentials as presented in Philippians 3:5-6.
 ☐ Read "Savor God's Truth" for Chapter 6.
 ☐ Complete all parts of the "Season Your Life" section as part of your spiritual preparation for teaching this lesson on the experiential knowledge of Christ.
 ☐ Before the group meets again for Bible study, telephone your members. Let them know that you care about them. Be a good listener. Look for specific ways you can encourage them in their pursuit of Christ.

Group Participation
 ☐ Have group members share their answers to question 2 from "Simmer These Thoughts." Ask, "Would anyone be willing to share a distinct difference that you see in your pursuits of life since you have come to know Jesus as your Saviour?"
 ☐ Have group members share their answers to question 3 from "Simmer These Thoughts." Ask, "When do you think righteousness is a 'stumbling block'? When do you think righteousness is a 'stepping-stone'?"
 ☐ Have group members share their answers to all parts of question 4 from "Simmer These Thoughts" except the personal confrontation question.
 ☐ Discuss answers to question 5 from the "Simmer These Thoughts" section. Ask, "What is the difference between 'experiential' knowledge and 'intellectual' knowledge? How can experiencing Christ's resurrection and His suffering cause us to know Christ more intimately and more genuinely?"
 ☐ Discuss answers to question 6 from the "Simmer These Thoughts" section.
 ☐ Have group members share their answers to question 7 from "Simmer These Thoughts," but exclude the personal confrontation questions. Ask, "How can our achievements keep us from persevering in the footrace of life?"

☐ Discuss answers to question 8 from the "Simmer These Thoughts" section.

☐ Tell group members to choose a verse from Philippians 3:4-16, 20-21 that best summarizes the session, then to explain their choices to the others.

☐ Ask, "In what ways have you been challenged to pursue the full, experiential knowledge of Christ through this lesson? In what ways are you experiencing more joy because of this study from the Book of Philippians?"

☐ Close with prayer.

❧ *THE LEADER'S RECIPE 7* ❧

Objective
To help group members discover how to experience peace with God, with others, and within themselves.

Personal Preparation
  ☐ Complete the "Simmer These Thoughts" section for Chapter 7.
  ☐ Read "Savor God's Truth" for Chapter 7.
  ☐ Complete all parts of "Season Your Life" as part of your spiritual preparation for teaching this lesson on how to experience peace with God, others, and self.
  ☐ Spend time praying specifically for each group member. Praise the Lord for evidences of new joy that have developed among group members as a result of this Bible study. Pray that this week's lesson will cause a life change for each member.
  ☐ Are you experiencing the peace of God through your relationship with the God of peace? Is there anyone with whom you need to be reconciled? What will you resolve to do about it before leading this lesson?

Group Participation
  ☐ Have group members share answers for question 1 from the "Simmer These Thoughts" section. Ask, "Can someone explain what relationship there is between standing firm in the Lord and experiencing joy?"
  ☐ Have group members share their answers to question 3, except for the personal confrontation part.
  ☐ Have group members share their answers to question 4. Ask, "What should be our response to disagreements among Christians that we know?"
  ☐ Discuss answers to question 5 from "Simmer These Thoughts." Say, "If anyone is not sure if his or her name is written in the 'Book of Life,' I will be glad to talk with you when we finish today."
  ☐ Discuss answers to questions 6 and 7 from "Simmer These Thoughts."
  ☐ Have group members share their answers to question 8 from "Simmer These Thoughts." Read Philippians 4:7 aloud from the *New International Version* or the *New American Standard Bible*. Ask, "What visual imagery does the word 'guard' bring to your mind?" After group members share their thoughts, challenge them to mentally apply this word picture to the way in which God guards their hearts and minds with His peace.

☐ Have group members share their answers to question 9 from the "Simmer These Thoughts" section.

☐ Have group members share their answers to question 10. Ask, "How does Philippians 4:8 relate to our choices of movies, television shows, reading material, and so on?"

☐ Direct group members to choose a verse from Philippians 4:1-9 that seems to summarize the session, then to explain their choices to the others.

☐ Close with prayer. As members of the group leave, be available in case someone wants to talk to you about his or her name being in the "Book of Life."

❧ *THE LEADER'S RECIPE 8* ❧

Objective
To help group members experience the full power of Christ within their lives.

Personal Preparation
☐ Complete the "Simmer These Thoughts" section for Chapter 8.
☐ Read "Savor God's Truth" for Chapter 8.
☐ Complete all parts of the "Season Your Life" section as part of your spiritual preparation for teaching this lesson on the full power of Christ.

Group Preparation
☐ Have group members share their answers to questions 1 and 2 from "Simmer These Thoughts."
☐ Discuss answers to question 3 from "Simmer These Thoughts." Ask, "Can anyone share a time when God directly supplied your needs by working through someone in your life?"
☐ Read 2 Corinthians 9:6-8 aloud. Ask, "What is the relationship between joy and giving? What are the results?"
☐ Have group members share their answers to question 6 from the "Simmer These Thoughts" section. If group members do not bring it out in their discussion, emphasize that verse 19 refers to "all" our needs. Have group members name the various needs that "all" might include.
☐ Have group members discuss questions 7 and 8 from "Simmer These Thoughts."
☐ Tell group members to choose one verse from Philippians 4:10-23 that best summarizes the session.
☐ Ask, "What changes in your life have you experienced because of this study?"
☐ Ask for prayer requests. Close with prayer.